THE
FORGOTTEN
ART OF
FLOWER
COOKERY

Leona Woodring Smith

Drawings by Liz Thompson

HARPER & ROW, PUBLISHERS

New York, Evanston, San Francisco, London

Grateful acknowledgment is made to the publishers for permission to use excerpts from T. S. Eliot and Emily Dickinson. The lines from "The pedigree of honey" are taken from *The Complete Poems of Emily Dickinson* edited by Thomas H. Johnson, published by Little, Brown and Company. The lines from T. S. Eliot's "The Waste Land" are reprinted by permission of Harcourt Brace Jovanovich, Inc.

FIRST EDITION

Designed by Lydia Link

Library of Congress Cataloging in Publication Data

Smith, Leona Woodring.
  The forgotten art of flower cookery.
  1. Cookery (Flowers) I. Title.
TX814.5.F5S64   641.6   73–4124
ISBN 0–06–013934–X

*To my parents, who inspired me with a childhood
filled with flowers and fragrant memories,*
AND
*to my husband, daughter, and close friends for
their patience, culinary help, and encouragement
in the research and writing of this book.*

Contents

Acknowledgments

I wish to express my appreciation for the kind cooperation received while conducting research at the following:

The Department of Agriculture, Washington, D.C.

The Library of Congress, Washington, D.C.

The National Library of Medicine of the National Institutes of Health, Bethesda, Maryland

The American Horticultural Society, Washington, D.C.

The Philadelphia Horticultural Society, Philadelphia, Pa.

National Poison Control Center, Department of Food and Drug Control, Washington, D.C.

Dumbarton Oaks Garden Library of Research, Washington, D.C.

U.S. National Arboretum Library, Washington, D.C.

The Garden Center, Hugh Taylor Birch State Park, Fort Lauderdale, Florida

Public libraries everywhere.

THE FORGOTTEN ART OF FLOWER COOKERY

Introduction

In the seventeenth century if you had met a maiden gathering flowers along a country lane, her explanation might have gone like this:

"We've made many fine salads this summer with nasturtiums, borage, and roses; tonight I am planning a stew with marigolds.

"Work in the stillroom goes well this year. We've had good crops of day lilies, lavender, and gillyflowers [carnations] for our medicines. Uncle John should get along well this winter for we distilled many jars of violet water for his gout. Have you noticed how beautiful the roses are? We've made two dozen crocks of rose-petal preserves."

Flowers have long been treasured for much more than their beauty. They were candied, pickled, dried, stewed, or their essence was captured in waters and oils. Truly a forgotten art worth reviving!

A box of candied roses and violets started me on six years of research. Once I discovered that flowers had been cultivated "for medicinal purposes and to please the gourmet's palate as well" I was committed—far too interested to quit. As the history and romance of flower cookery enveloped me I constantly urged

1

my garden to grow faster so I could try out my new inspirations using the flavor, aroma, and beauty of flowers.

Food has always been of crucial interest to all mankind. Providing enjoyment to both body and mind, cookery has been an enticing art for hundreds of years. Men such as Confucius, known for their wisdom and philosophy, have recorded their culinary interests. Chrysanthemums were used as food in his day, and Xenophon, the Greek historian, tells us that the Persians included nasturtiums in their diet about 400 B.C.

Eating and drinking were the chief pleasures of the Greeks and Romans when they weren't making war, and their banquets often lasted for days. Detailed accounts of the luxury of the times tell of rose petals in the wines and stews and violets in the cakes.

The seventeenth century saw a great advance in Europe in the art of cookery. It was enthusiastically pursued and everyone who could afford it became interested in food. Preparing food was no easy matter. You could not phone the butcher, the baker, or the greengrocer from the bridge table and serve the family dinner thirty minutes after arriving home. There was no refrigeration, no electrical equipment or commercial aids. High seasonings and artistic preparation were the basis of culinary masterpieces. Thus flowers, herbs, and spices were heavily relied upon.

The Industrial Revolution brought new techniques to the cooking world—labor-saving devices, methods of preservation, and even instant cooking. Flowers, herbs, and spices went out of fashion. Rebellion against tradition produced generations attuned to mechanical cuisine; everything was perfectly measured and cooked and ready for instant use. The days of "provincial cookery" were over.

But nothing is final. The pendulum keeps swinging. Today's computerized world of synthetics seems to press upon us too closely, too routinely; and so we find ourselves again returning to the use of eyes, nose, and palate to seek pleasure in the enjoyment of food. There have always been a large number of true gourmets who never turned off their God-given senses; this book is for the multitude who are rediscovering beauty in food—and the forgotten art of flower cookery.

Note to the Reader

Whenever possible use garden-grown flowers. The old-fashioned varieties are more desirable than greenhouse varieties, which often have been crossbred until they offer little fragrance or taste and tend to be tough. The more fragrant the flower, the more flavor it offers!

Flowers are best gathered in the cool of the morning, washed and refrigerated until used. However, flowers to be dried for teas and winter use should be picked in the heat of the day when they are free from dew.

Fresh flowers are used in all recipes in this book unless otherwise noted.

All flowers should be washed thoroughly (but gently!), drained, and stored between layers of paper towels so they are dry before you proceed with recipes.

One other general comment: "salt and pepper to taste" is usually indicated throughout this book. This is a highly personal point and every cook of any experience will handle it in accordance with his or her personal taste.

During my lectures I always emphasize the need to use a good French dressing on salads containing flowers because their delicate taste is easily masked by a heavy, oily dressing. During the years many people have come to me and asked for the recipe I consider a good one. I'd like to include it here.

"GOOD" FRENCH DRESSING

About 1/2 cup

 6 tablespoons salad oil
 2 tablespoons wine vinegar and/or lemon juice
 ¼ teaspoon salt
 1 garlic clove (optional)
Pinch of curry powder
Pinch of dry mustard
Big pinch of pepper (freshly ground, preferably)
Dash of Tabasco

Place in a screw-top jar and shake vigorously for 30 seconds immediately before using.

Salad ingredients should be perfectly dry (but crisp) so the dressing adheres.

Do not store dressing in the refrigerator but make fresh frequently.

CANDIED FLOWERS

Imitation was unknown to cooks of the seventeenth and eighteenth centuries. The candied flowers used to enhance cakes and other desserts were of natural origin. Candy jars on the pantry shelf probably contained candied (or crystallized) violets, rose petals, mint leaves, tiny yellow balls of mimosa, or blue stars of borage.

There are several methods for candying flowers. Here are the two simplest but most successful ways.

Egg white
Small camel's-hair brush

(continued)

Fresh petals, well washed and dried
Tweezers
Granulated sugar

Beat the white of an egg until slightly frothy. With the brush paint both sides of the petals (or whole flowers) and using the tweezers dip into very fine granulated sugar. Place on waxed paper to dry.

Sugar syrup
Tweezers
Fresh petals, well washed and dried
Granulated sugar

Make a syrup of 1 cup sugar and 1/2 cup water. Boil until it spins a thread. Cool to room temperature. Using tweezers dip the petals (or whole flowers) into the syrup; gently shake off the excess and dip into fine granulated sugar. Place on waxed paper to dry.

For a prettier effect you may color the sugar the same as the flower by adding a couple of drops of food coloring and blending well. Use about 2-3 drops to 3-4 tablespoons sugar. Thoroughly mix and allow to dry out for 2-3 hours before using, stirring occasionally.

Lilac flowers should be broken from the stem and each floweret candied individually.

Rose petals may be candied individually or tiny roses may be used whole. Stand in a warm dry place and be sure they are thoroughly dried before storing.

Borage, violets, or orange, lemon, or lime blossoms may be candied whole.

Gardenia petals and mint leaves should be handled individually.

Borage

"I, borage, bring thee courage" is an old saying of the English, who got it from the Romans, who most likely got it from the Greeks. Borage is pronounced to rhyme with courage and is believed to be a corruption of that word. Since the days of early Greece men believed borage had "the power to drive away melancholy," according to Pliny, the Roman naturalist. Courage in adversity is intended, not physical courage. Many credit it with giving physical courage too, however, probably because of its high content of potassium and other minerals. It has long been considered what we today call a wonder drug.

Native to the Mediterranean, where it still grows wild on the hillsides of Sicily, it is believed to have been brought to America by early colonists, who always carried seeds with them to plant in the New World. Seeds of courage certainly were needed.

Borage flourishes in ordinary soil and no plant is more easily grown. It reseeds itself year after year and thus frequently is found growing untended in out-of-the-way places. Nestled in rough gray foliage are clusters of heavenly blue flowers—each perfectly star-shaped and breathtaking. The beauty of these magnificent flowers has been preserved over and over in floral paintings and needlework for centuries.

In the garden borage offers beauty and fragrance, and in the kitchen it adds a third delight—its special flavor. The honeyed cucumber-like taste of borage, combined with its perfect beauty and heavenly sky-blue color, has enhanced dishes for centuries. It is equally at home in cold drinks or fresh salads, garnishing the soup pot, or lending its decorative touch to game or fish. Borage is the only "true blue culinary flower."

Borage flowers are especially pretty in ice molds, or in individual ice cubes for party punches, etc.

A well-chilled sauterne, served in a clear crystal wine glass, is further enhanced by floating a borage flower in it.

Top grapefruit with a borage flower, or combine grapefruit sections with borage blossoms in salad greens.

Potato salad becomes festive when a few blue borage stars are tucked in, and borage leaves line the salad bowl. Likewise the blue of borage combines nicely with hard-boiled eggs in salad.

Top cold soups with a dab of sour cream and a blue star.

Fresh peas take on a special look if a few borage flowers are tucked in before serving. Boiled potatoes, rolled in butter and sprinkled with finely chopped borage leaves and topped with a few flowers, have a new look.

The bright blue stars are dramatic with cottage cheese, and the flavors marry well.

Add a few of the colorful flowers to a platter of corned beef and cabbage before serving.

Our great-great-grandmothers used these blue flowers as a garnish for lemonade.

Candied borage flowers are most attractive on a white-frosted cake. See page 5 for directions.

Thoroughly but gently wash the flowers and drain on a paper towel. They may be refrigerated on a damp paper towel until you are ready to use them.

CIDER CUP WITH BORAGE

12 servings

1½ quarts cider
 4 ounces dry sherry
 ¼ cup sugar
 1 lemon studded with 12 cloves and cut into quarters
 1 handful of borage leaves, plus flowers for garnish
 6 ounces brandy
 1 cup orange juice
 1 cup soda water (optional)

Place all ingredients (except soda water) in a container and chill about 2-3 hours. Strain into a punch bowl, adding soda water if desired. In a ring mold with about 1/2 inch of water invert 12-18 borage flowers and freeze. Then fill the mold with ice water so as not to disturb that which is already solid. Freeze until ready to add to punch bowl. Surround the bowl with borage flowers and leaves.

CLARET CUP WITH BORAGE

About 10 servings

  1 bottle claret
  ½ cup cognac
  2 tablespoons sugar
  1 sliced orange, unpeeled
  1 sliced lemon, unpeeled
6-8 borage leaves, crushed
2-3 cups soda water, chilled
  1 stem of borage and flowers for garnish

(*continued*)

In a large container place claret, cognac, sugar, orange, lemon, and borage. Let stand for 2 hours. Chill. Strain into a punch bowl and add soda water and an ice mold containing borage. (See previous recipe for method.) Additional borage may surround the punch bowl and flowers may be picked off to garnish each cup as it is served.

PIMM'S CUP COOLER

Makes 1 drink

3 ounces Pimm's Cup, No. 1
2 teaspoons sugar
2 borage flowers and leaves plus 1 flower for garnish
Juice of 1 lime and squeezed hull
1 ounce dry gin

Reserving 1 flower for garnish, place remaining ingredients into a cocktail shaker with crushed ice and shake well. Strain into a chilled glass and garnish with a flower.

Borage as a garnish for Pimm's Cup was replaced over the years by a curl of cucumber peel—cucumbers being more accessible. But some niceties are worth the effort, and the delicacy of borage as the garnish for Pimm's Cup served in a chilled pewter mug seems a must.

BLENDER BORAGE SOUP

6 servings

2 cups chicken broth
1 cup buttermilk
1½ tablespoons chopped onion
1½ tablespoons lemon juice

Salt and pepper
  6 borage leaves
  2 cucumbers
  1 cup sour cream
  6 borage flowers

Put the broth and buttermilk into a blender with the onion, lemon juice, salt and pepper, borage leaves, and cucumbers (peeled, seeded, and quartered), and blend well. Add the sour cream and blend again. Chill well. In serving garnish each individual bowl with a blue borage star flower.

BORAGE-GRAPE MOLD

6-8 servings

  1¾ cups water
   1 package lime gelatin
   6 borage leaves
   2 cups seedless grapes
   1 cup drained crushed pineapple
12-18 borage flowers

Heat 1 cup of the water and dissolve the gelatin; let stand to cool. Place remaining 3/4 cup water in the blender with borage leaves for 90 seconds. Combine with the gelatin and stir until evenly mixed, then add the grapes and crushed pineapple and stir again. Chill until syrupy (egg-white consistency).

(continued)

Spoon 3-4 tablespoons into the bottom of a mold, place half the borage flowers in the mold face down so they will make a pretty picture when unmolded, and allow to set firmly before adding the remaining flowers and gelatin mixture. Chill until firm.

FOURTH OF JULY SALAD

6-8 servings

 1 **package plain gelatin**
 2 **cups water**
 2 **tablespoons lemon juice**
 2 **tablespoons sugar**
 Salt and pepper to taste
 1 **cup chopped cucumber (peeled and seeded first)**
 ¾ **cup chopped radishes**
 2 **tablespoons grated onion**
15-18 **borage flowers**

Sprinkle the gelatin on 1/2 cup of the water to soften. Heat the remaining water and combine. Stir in the lemon juice, sugar, salt, and pepper. Blend well and place in the refrigerator until thickened (like egg white) and then gently fold in the cucumber, radishes, onion, and borage flowers and pour into a mold. Chill until firm. Unmold on salad greens and add a few additional flowers.

Carnation

Carnations . . . pinks . . . clove pinks . . . gillyflowers. The carnation has had a dickens of a time establishing its name.

"Gillyflower" was probably a corruption of the old French word for clove, *girofle*, and clovelike they are in both fragrance and flavor. "Pinks" was most likely a corruption of *pinct*, which means pinked or scalloped, the contour of the carnation's petals. The original flowers were flesh-toned (or pink) in coloring and the color pink got its name from the flower, not vice versa. "Carnation" originally was a word for flesh tone or color (*carnatio*) and when Linnaeus in the eighteenth century classified the flowers with Latin names the "pinct" became "carnation" (flesh-colored flower).

According to Christian legend carnations first bloomed where Mary's tears fell on the earth as she walked along the road to Calvary. Faith in the protective power of anything connected with Mary gave carnations immediate popularity. They have gone in and out of fashion many times since then. They were popular during the Renaissance as festive decorations, and their spicy flavor was added to wine for the festivities. Today the carnation is an ingredient of several wines and of the liqueur Chartreuse.

Carnations reached another peak of popularity in the eighteenth century when the Dutch started cultivating them on a large scale. Throughout Europe growing carnations became a pastime for rich and poor alike. Slowly they acquired great symbolic significance. Few other flowers have been so representative to so many people for so many different reasons:

French nobles wore them as they marched to the guillotine.

McKinley adopted the scarlet carnation for his presidential campaign.

Dyed green they make their yearly mark for the Irish.

Austrian youths pin them on their hats to show they are in love.

The carnation is the emblem for Mother's Day.

The carnation almost saved the life of Marie Antoinette when a would-be rescuer smuggled a message to her concealed in the petals of a carnation. Alas, the plot failed.

For best results in the kitchen choose carnations grown in the garden as they are more tender and have more flavor than the greenhouse varieties.

Few flowers equal carnations for sweetness, but when working with them, as with other multipetaled flowers (such as chrysanthemums, marigolds, roses), hold the flower, pull the petals en masse from the stem, and clip off the heels, or white bottoms, from the petals, as this point of attachment may produce a bitter taste.

Always wash the flowers thoroughly but gently.

CARNATION VINEGAR

Prepare petals and place in a pint jar. Cover with a good cider vinegar and let stand 10 days. Strain and use vinegar on salads —especially good on fruit salad.

CARNATION SALAD

4-6 servings

Bibb lettuce, 1 or 2 heads
½ cucumber, peeled, quartered, and sliced very thin
½ cup carnation petals
1 tablespoon minced parsley

Combine the following ingredients for the dressing and toss with salad ingredients at the table:

3 tablespoons oil
1 tablespoon rose vinegar (or carnation—see above)
½ teaspoon lemon juice
Pinch curry powder
1 teaspoon honey
Salt and pepper to taste

PICKLED CARNATIONS

1 pint

Fill a pint jar with prepared, chopped carnation petals.

    1 cup cider vinegar
    ½ cup sugar
    1 stick cinnamon
    Pinch mace
    Salt and pepper to taste

Bring the above ingredients to a boil for 3 minutes. Let stand off heat for 30 minutes, remove the cinnamon stick, and pour over the petals. Cover and shake the jar gently. Let stand for 48 hours before using.

Very nice to garnish ham or lamb.

CANDIED CARNATIONS

See page 5.

CARNATION STRAWBERRY JAM

8-10 medium glasses

    2½ cups crushed fresh strawberries
     2 cups chopped carnation petals
     2 tablespoons lemon juice
    ½ teaspoon ground cinnamon
     7 cups sugar
    ½ bottle fruit pectin (Certo)

Combine all the ingredients but the pectin; blend and bring to a full boil for 1 minute, stirring constantly. Then add the half bottle of pectin and bring to a full boil for one minute, stirring constantly. Remove from the heat, skim off the foam and pour into the jelly glasses.

CARNATION DESSERT JELLY

6 servings

Prepare 1 package raspberry gelatin according to directions. Blend into it:

½ teaspoon rose water
½ teaspoon almond extract
½ teaspoon cinnamon

Chill until partially thickened, about the consistency of egg whites, then add:

1 cup chopped carnation petals
½ cup chopped walnuts

Chill until firm. Serve with whipped cream to which a few drops of rose water have been added.

CARNATION CREPES

4-6 servings

Prepare basic crêpe batter:

1 cup all-purpose flour
Salt

(continued)

1   egg plus 1 yolk
1   cup beer
1   tablespoon melted butter

Sift the flour and salt into a bowl. Add the egg and extra yolk and about half of the beer. Blend until smooth. Add the rest of the beer and the melted butter. Beat well, and allow to rest for 2 hours.

Cook the crêpes and place them in a stack on a clean cloth or plate.

FILLING

1   package frozen raspberries
Pulp of 1 orange
1   tablespoon grated orange peel
1   cup chopped carnation petals
2   tablespoons kirsch
2   tablespoons Grand Marnier
2   tablespoons currant jelly
2   teaspoons cornstarch dissolved in 1 tablespoon cold water

Bring the raspberries, orange, orange peel, carnations, kirsch, Grand Marnier, and currant jelly to a boil. Add cornstarch and stir until thickened.

Place some of this sauce on each crêpe and roll. Dust with powdered sugar and serve with whipped cream.

CARNATION DESSERT OMELET

2 servings

1½ teaspoons butter
4 eggs
Salt and pepper
1 tablespoon orange juice
1 tablespoon sugar
⅓ cup carnation petals
2 tablespoons of your favorite liqueur
Powdered sugar

Put the butter in an omelet pan to melt. Beat with a fork the eggs, salt and pepper, orange juice, and sugar. When the butter is about to smoke tip the pan to coat the sides. Pour in the egg mixture and tip in a circular manner so the eggs cover the whole pan and cook evenly.

The bottom should be golden and the center still soft when finished. Before folding over, place the carnation petals in the center.

I like to chop the carnation petals first and let them stand in Grand Marnier (or other liqueur) while I prepare the omelet. Any remaining liqueur after spooning the carnations onto the omelet I usually dribble over the folded omelet, which I then sprinkle lightly with powdered sugar.

CARNATION FRITTERS

4-6 servings

½ bottle beer (6 ounces)
½ cup flour
Salt

Blend well and let stand 3 hours or more.

Marinate 1 cup carnation petals in Chartreuse (or lemon juice) for 15 minutes. Drain, dust with flour, dip into batter, and cook in deep oil (375°F.) until golden.

Sprinkle with powdered sugar or cinnamon sugar and serve immediately.

Excellent with after-dinner coffee.

CARNATION SAUCE FOR DESSERTS

Makes 1 1/2 cups sauce

½ cup currant jelly
1 cup carnation petals
¾ cup raspberries (strawberries may be substituted)
½ cup sugar
1 teaspoon lemon juice
½ teaspoon cinnamon
1 teaspoon cornstarch

Place the first 6 ingredients in a blender and blend for 60 seconds. Pour into a saucepan, add the cornstarch, and cook over low heat, stirring constantly, until thick and clear.

Use on ice cream, cake, pudding, etc. May be served hot or cold.

CARNATION-CHERRIES JUBILEE

6 servings

1 fourteen-and-a-half-ounce jar Bing cherries, pitted
1 stick cinnamon
¼ cup sugar
1 teaspoon lemon juice
1 cup chopped carnation petals (preferably dark red)
5 tablespoons brandy

Place the juice from the pitted cherries in a saucepan with cinnamon stick, sugar, lemon juice, and carnation petals. Boil for 3 minutes, stirring constantly. Remove from heat, add cherries and 2 tablespoons of the brandy, blend, and let stand.

To serve, remove the cinnamon stick, reheat the sauce, and pour into a sauceboat. In a separate pan heat remaining 3 tablespoons brandy, ignite and pour over the sauce, and carry to the table flaming. Serve immediately on vanilla ice cream.

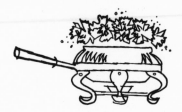

PINK PIE

6 servings

Dough for a 9-inch shell and lattice crust
3 cups rhubarb, cut in small pieces
1 cup chopped red and pink carnation petals
3½ tablespoons flour
1½ cups sugar
3 tablespoons butter

(continued)

   2 tablespoons strawberry jelly
   1 tablespoon rose water
   ½ teaspoon cinnamon
   ½ teaspoon lemon juice
   ½ teaspoon lemon peel

Line a 9-inch pie pan with the pastry dough. In a bowl combine the rhubarb and carnations. Sift the flour over them, blend well, add sugar, blend again, and pour into pastry shell.

In a saucepan melt the butter and jelly. Remove from the heat. Add rose water, cinnamon, lemon juice and peel. Blend well and dribble over ingredients in pastry shell.

Put a lattice crust over the top and bake at 450°F. for 15 minutes. Turn the heat down to 325° for 25 minutes more.

Serve warm topped with whipped cream flavored with a few drops of rose water.

Chives

"Chives"—a word of magic among chefs! Always plural, as the chive multiplies rapidly to become a mass of bulbs.

Legend tells us that the alliums (garlic, onions, leeks, and chives) sprang up from the footsteps of Satan; they have been adding gusto to foods since Biblical days. Before the Christian era they were apparently known to the Chinese (about 2500 B.C.), who used them to halt bleeding and as an antidote for poisoning. Tomb drawings show that great respect was paid to chives by the Greeks and Romans. Whether Columbus brought them to this country, or first tasted them here, remains unresolved, but the overall acceptance of this delicate herb cannot be disputed.

Chives are credited with stimulating the appetite, strengthening the stomach, lowering blood pressure, providing a good source of calcium and iron, and like all alliums are beneficial to the kidneys. Some records even credit them with being mildly antibiotic.

You needn't be a gardener to raise chives. Many a housewife brings home from the supermarket potted chives to bloom and flourish on the kitchen window sill. They do equally well in the city or country, requiring only water and sunshine in return for their culinary delights.

Whoever heard of vichyssoise without chives? Picture then

the graceful addition of a purple-blue blossom to grace the center—impressive eye appeal plus flavor. Chive flowers add eye appeal to many other dishes also. Picture:

> Cottage cheese with chopped chive leaves and purplish buds.
> Cold soup topped with a dab of sour cream with the flower midst chopped leaves as garnish.
> The contrast of the golden hue of carrots with the minced flower and stems.
> Rice, stuffed eggs, omelets, sauces, and cucumber, and other salads accented with chives' purplish hues.

Use your own imagination in blending colors, textures, and flavors. Chives are the mildest of the allium family, but the flowers reflect the growing conditions and vary in strength. Always use young tender flowers; taste a petal or two before blending into other ingredients and use accordingly. Always wash the flowers thoroughly but gently, and dry carefully before using.

CHIVE OMELET

2 servings

Use two eggs plus 1/2 teaspoon of water per person. Never cook more than 4 eggs at one time.

 1 tablespoon butter
 4 eggs

1 teaspoon water
1 teaspoon chopped chive leaves
1 or 2 chive flowers (taste petals for strength and use
   accordingly)
Salt and pepper

Place butter in an omelet pan; when foaming add the eggs
and water (beaten about 30 strokes) and keep moving the pan in
a circular motion until the liquid is set. Before folding over, add
the chive leaves and petals and salt and pepper to taste.

Chicken stock may be used in place of water for added
richness.

POLKA-DOT POTATO CAKE

2-3 servings

4 tablespoons bacon drippings
3 medium baking potatoes
1 tablespoon chopped chive leaves
1 or 2 chive flowers (pull petals from the stem and check
   for strength)
Salt and pepper to taste

Place the bacon drippings in a skillet to melt. Peel and grate
the potatoes and combine the other ingredients with them.
Spread evenly in the skillet and cook, covered, over medium heat
until the bottom is nicely browned. Loosen around the edges
carefully, turn over, and brown the other side.

CHIVE SHRIMP

4 servings

1 pound raw shrimp
1 cup dry white wine
¼ teaspoon salt
3 tablespoons butter
2 tablespoons flour
¾ cup light cream
4 tablespoons finely chopped raw mushrooms
1 tablespoon chopped chive leaves
1 tablespoon chive flower petals

Shell and devein the shrimp and cut into bite-size pieces. Place the wine, salt, and shrimp in a saucepan and simmer for 4-5 minutes. Drain immediately and reserve 1/2 cup of the liquid.

Melt the butter in a pan, blend in the flour, and gradually add the reserved liquid and cream, stirring slowly until the sauce is smooth and thickened. Add the shrimp, mushrooms, and chive leaves and petals and simmer another 2-3 minutes. Serve on toast points.

Chrysanthemum

The shadows, lengthening, stretch at noon;
The fields are stripped, the groves are dumb;
The first-flowers greet the icy moon,—
Then blooms the bright Chrysanthemum.

ANONYMOUS

It seems quite appropriate that the sharp sting of autumn should bring forth the chrysanthemum. In the language of flowers it signifies love and truth—two virtues which if they are to bloom in the world around us must endure a climate oftentimes chilly and harsh.

The Chinese maintain, and history seems to support them, that the chrysanthemum originated in China. As early as 500 B.C., Confucius wrote of their "yellow glory." It was the favorite flower of the Mandarins and eventually became a familiar emblem in temples, on porcelain, in textiles, wood and metal work. The Chinese cherished the flower and sought to confine the "yellow glory" to the mainland, but eventually it found its way to Japan.

Since the chrysanthemum was introduced to Japan in the fourth century, it has become one of the country's most popular emblems. It is the national flower and appears on the flag as an emblematic blossom with 16 petals radiating out from a central disc.

In A.D. 797 it attracted the attention of the Mikado and was designated as the official emblem. He wrote poems about it and created the Order of the Chrysanthemum, the highest honor he could bestow. For years the flower was permitted to be cultivated only in the imperial gardens and those of the nobility.

Both the Chinese and the Japanese believe that a chrysanthemum petal in the bottom of a wine glass promotes longevity, and the Chinese also claim it has the power to turn white hair black.

Along with other secrets of the Orient, chrysanthemums were brought to Europe by merchants in the early eighteenth century. Several varieties found their way to England by way of France and Holland. Small-flowered plants became a staple of English gardens, and in 1859 a million potted chrysanthemums arranged in tiers provided the floral decoration for a commemorative celebration at London's Crystal Palace.

Even the regal chrysanthemum has had a few black sheep in its family. Rumor has it that some chrysanthemum kin, under the names of corn marigold, oxeye daisy and feverfew, went the way of weeds in the countryside of old England.

Although no exact date is given for its American debut, the cultivation of the chrysanthemum in this country was undoubtedly furthered by Mrs. Alpheus Hardy, wife of a Boston sea captain. In 1892 Mrs. Hardy was sailing aboard her husband's ship when he discovered a young Japanese stowaway. She intervened, was instrumental in the boy's sailing to Boston, and later sent him to college. When he returned to Japan, he sent her a batch of chrysanthemum cuttings. They quickly acquired a choice place in the gardens and hearts of Americans. Careful and judicious breeding has produced hundreds of species in many shapes and colors.

Long regarded as the queen of the fall garden, today they are available all year long. A potted chrysanthemum in the kitchen window will provide a cook with an ever-present gourmet touch. I make no claim that it will increase longevity or reduce gray hair, but I do know the chrysanthemum can be as delightful to the palate as it is to the eye.

TO PREPARE CHRYSANTHEMUMS:

Always wash the flowers thoroughly but gently, and allow to drain and dry before proceeding.

Grasp the stem firmly with your right hand, and with your other hand pull the petals (en masse) from the head. Then take kitchen shears and cut off the white (sometimes greenish) heels by which the petals were attached to the flower head, as this part can produce a bitter taste if not removed.

Chrysanthemums have a subtle, aromatic, piquant flavor and offer an interesting texture for salads and main dishes.

The petals may be used raw, blanched, or seasoned by standing in salt water for 15-20 minutes. I like the crispness of using them raw, but those who prefer a milder flavor may use one of the other methods.

Guard against overcooking chrysanthemums, as they lose their texture.

CHRYSANTHEMUM FISH CHOWDER

8-10 servings

A favorite of the men—especially if made with "his catch" and "his flowers."

½ cup olive oil
½ cup minced onion
 1 clove garlic, minced

(continued)

½ cup minced celery
2 tablespoons minced parsley

In a deep soup pot cook the above until tender but not browned, then add:

1 cup chicken broth
1½ cups clam juice
1 bay leaf
½ teaspoon thyme
1½ cups cubed potatoes
½ cup cubed carrots
1 quart water
Salt and pepper to taste
2 cups fish fillets in chunks

Boil gently all ingredients except fish approximately 15 minutes, then add fish fillets and simmer 10 minutes more.
Remove from heat and stir in:

2 tablespoons Madeira wine
½ cup finely shredded lettuce
⅔ cup chrysanthemum petals

Serve at once.

PEKING TURKEY CHOWDER

10-12 servings

4 tablespoons butter
½ cup chopped onion
2 tablespoons chopped green pepper
¾ cup chopped celery

2 cups diced potatoes
1½ cups corn (cut from the cob or canned)
5 cups turkey stock
2 chicken bouillon cubes
Pinch of tarragon
2½ cups cubed cooked turkey
1 cup light cream
1½ tablespoons minced parsley
1 cup chrysanthemum petals (bronze is nice in the fall,
     other times yellow or white)
Salt and pepper to taste

Put the butter in a skillet and sauté the onion until translucent. Place in a kettle the pepper, celery, potatoes, corn, turkey
stock, bouillon cubes, and tarragon. Mix well and cook gently
for 15 minutes.

Add the turkey and cream. Simmer over low heat for another 10 minutes. Add the parsley and chrysanthemum petals
and let stand off the heat until ready to serve. Additional stock
and cream may be added in equal proportion, if desired. Stir
gently and serve. Reheat if necessary.

CHRYSANTHEMUM SALAD

5-6 servings

¼ cup white-wine vinegar
3 tablespoons honey
3 tablespoons lemon juice
1 teaspoon chopped fresh tarragon
Petals from 3 large chrysanthemums
½ cup olive oil
Lettuce and watercress
Salt and pepper to taste

(continued)

Mix together vinegar, honey, lemon juice, and tarragon. Marinate the petals for 30 minutes. Add oil and blend well. Add sufficient lettuce and watercress to the salad bowl for 6 people and toss with the petal mixture, salt, and pepper. Serve immediately.

Bronze petals form a nice color contrast for this dish, but you may choose any shade in keeping with other foods being served.

WHIPPED-CREAM DRESSING
(For Fruit Salad)

Makes 1 3/4 cups

⅓ cup sugar
1 tablespoon flour
1 egg, beaten
1½ tablespoons salad oil
2½ tablespoons lemon and/or orange juice
½ cup pineapple juice
¼ cup heavy cream, whipped
Petals of 1 or 2 chrysanthemums (approximately 1 cup)

Combine dry ingredients in a saucepan; add remaining ingredients except cream and chrysanthemum petals.

Cook over low heat until thickened, stirring constantly. Cool. Fold in whipped cream and chrysanthemum petals.

Use white, yellow, orchid, or bronze chrysanthemums, depending on the salad ingredients. Some people prefer to blanch the petals by covering them with boiling water for 60 seconds. I prefer the crispness of using them raw. Chopped candied ginger may be added.

HONG KONG SHRIMP SALAD

6 servings

1½ cups cooked shrimp
 1 cup diced cooked potatoes
 2 tablespoons capers
 1 cup chopped chrysanthemum petals
 ½ cup finely chopped celery
 2 tablespoons minced onion
 1 eight-ounce jar artichoke hearts, drained
Salt and pepper to taste
French dressing

Combine all the ingredients, toss in a good French dressing, and serve on lettuce or watercress.

CHRYSANTHEMUM SHRIMP SALAD

4-5 servings

 2 cups cooked shrimp, chopped
 ½ cup diced or crushed fresh pineapple
 ½ teaspoon chopped tarragon (preferably fresh)
 2 tablespoons capers
 ¼ cup French dressing
 ½ cup chrysanthemum petals (white or yellow)

Gently but thoroughly mix the above ingredients. Chill well and serve on crisp lettuce.

RAINBOW PICNIC SALAD SUPPER

10-12 servings

4 cups cooked chicken, cut in cubes
3 tablespoons orange juice
2 tablespoons vinegar
2 tablespoons salad oil
1 teaspoon salt

Combine above ingredients and refrigerate.
Prepare the following:

2½ cups cooked rice
1½ cups seedless grapes
1½ cups sliced celery
 1 cup pineapple tidbits (fresh or canned)
 1 cup mandarin oranges
 ¾ cup slivered almonds, toasted
1¼ cups mayonnaise
 ¼ cup yellow chrysanthemum petals
 ¼ cup sugar

Gently toss all ingredients together and refrigerate. Serve on lettuce. Additional chrysanthemum petals may be sprinkled over the top as a garnish, or whole flowers (small) may be placed around the mound of salad on the serving plate.

CHRYSANTHEMUM-ORANGE SALAD

6 servings

3 oranges, sectioned with membrane removed
1 avocado sliced
½ cup chrysanthemum petals
¼ cup slivered almonds

Combine above ingredients and toss with the following dressing:

½ cup mayonnaise
¼ cup honey
2 tablespoons tarragon vinegar
¼ teaspoon chopped fresh tarragon

If you are in a hurry any fruit salad takes on a glamorous touch when chrysanthemum petals are sprinkled over the top. Choose chrysanthemum color to accent the color of the fruit.

CHRYSANTHEMUM-SPINACH SALAD

6 servings

Wash, drain, and break into bite-size pieces 2 pounds spinach and 1-2 cups chrysanthemum petals. Toss with this dressing:

1 cup sour cream
½ cup honey
4 tablespoons vinegar
3 tablespoons horseradish
¼ teaspoon dry mustard
Salt and pepper to taste

AUTUMN EGG SALAD

4-6 servings

     6 hard-cooked eggs, diced
    ½ cup diced avocado
     4 or 5 pitted ripe black olives, chopped
    ¼ cup blue cheese
    ½ cup chopped chrysanthemum petals
     2 tablespoons lemon juice
    Mayonnaise to bind
    Salt and pepper to taste

Combine ingredients and allow to marinate one-half hour before serving on lettuce or watercress.

DYNASTY EGGS ON TOAST

6 servings

     5 tablespoons butter
     4 tablespoons flour
    2½ cups milk
    ¼ cup sherry
     2 tablespoons minced onion
     1 tablespoon minced parsley
    ½ teaspoon mustard
    ½ teaspoon salt
    ¼ teaspoon powdered ginger
    Pinch of pepper
     6 hard-boiled eggs, quartered
     1 cup cubed cooked ham
    12 pitted ripe olives, sliced
    ½ cup chrysanthemum petals

Put the butter into a skillet to melt, add the flour, and blend until smooth. Slowly add the milk, stirring constantly. Allow to simmer slowly a few minutes and then add the sherry, onion, parsley, mustard, salt, ginger, and pepper. Cook slowly until thickened and smooth. Then add the eggs, ham, olives, and chrysanthemum petals. Heat thoroughly and serve on toast.

STIR-FRIED CHICKEN A LA CHRYSANTHEMUM

4-5 servings

      2 chicken breasts
    ½ teaspoon salt
    ⅛ teaspoon ginger
      2 teaspoons cornstarch
1½ teaspoons sugar
      4 tablespoons oil
      2 tablespoons sherry
    ½ cup chicken stock
      2 tablespoons chopped scallions
    ¼ cup chrysanthemum petals

Bone chicken (this may be made easier by placing the chicken breasts in the freezer for 30-35 minutes, allowing the meat to become firm—not frozen) and cut into strips about 1 inch wide.

Combine dry ingredients and coat chicken slices. Heat oil to just below smoking point. Add chicken and move pieces briskly until firm and white. Add sherry, stock, and scallions. Stir until the liquid thickens; add the chrysanthemum petals and stir only until all ingredients have a clear glaze. Do not overcook petals or they will become bitter.

CHRYSANTHEMUM TURKEY THERMIDOR

6 servings

¼ cup butter
3 tablespoons flour
2 cups milk
1 teaspoon salt
¼ teaspoon pepper
½ teaspoon dry mustard
¾ cups grated American cheese
¼ cup sherry
2½ cups diced cooked turkey
1½ cups cooked peas
½ cup chrysanthemum petals

In a saucepan make a roux from butter (melted) and flour; add milk, salt, pepper, and mustard. Stir over heat until thick and smooth. Add cheese and sherry and stir until smooth. Fold in turkey, peas, and chrysanthemum petals, and stir gently over heat to the boiling point. Serve at once over rice or toast points.

SWEET POTATOES CHRYSANTHEMUM

6 servings

6 medium sweet potatoes
½ cup canned crushed pineapple
¼ cup honey
Salt and pepper to taste
2 tablespoons butter
½ teaspoon grated lemon rind
½ cup chopped chrysanthemum petals

Cook and mash the sweet potatoes. Add the pineapple, honey, salt and pepper, butter, lemon rind, and chrysanthemum petals.

Blend well, pour into a buttered casserole, and bake in a moderate oven (350°F.) 20-30 minutes.

CONFUCIUS SWEET POTATOES

3-4 servings

1 pound sweet potatoes or 1 seventeen-ounce can
1 cup orange juice
1 three-ounce package orange gelatin
¼ cup brown sugar
2 tablespoons butter
Salt and pepper to taste
1 cup yellow chrysanthemum petals

While sweet potatoes are cooking (if using raw potatoes) combine all other ingredients except petals. Simmer and stir for 5 minutes.

Place sweet potatoes in the syrup and let stand over the lowest possible heat for 15-20 minutes. Baste occasionally. Turn off heat, add petals, and baste until petals are glazed.

CHRYSANTHEMUM-EGG TEA SANDWICH SPREAD

For 2 dozen tea sandwiches

- 6 hard-cooked eggs (chopped)
- ¼ cup finely chopped celery
- 3 tablespoons minced onion
- 1 tablespoon minced green pepper
- ⅓ cup mayonnaise
- ½ teaspoon Worcestershire sauce
- Dash of Tabasco
- Salt and pepper to taste

Blend above ingredients and then fold in 1/2-3/4 cup chrysanthemum petals, any color you like, and refrigerate.

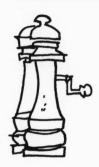

Clover

The common clover gained celebrity status during the days when St. Patrick roamed around Ireland and used it to demonstrate the unity of the Trinity to his listeners. He must have found a land where people so easily believed in mythical beings (leprechauns, elves, fairies, goblins, demons) a fertile place to sow seeds of faith. The peasants used to carry clover leaves in their shoes when crossing dark cornfields at night. When someone found a four-leaf clover it was regarded as a super symbol of the Trinity, with extraordinary powers of benevolence.

Belief in the lucky power of clover as a protector of love and heroism quickly spread, and even today people throughout the world accept the clover as a defense against bad luck and evil spirits. To dream of clover foretells fortune, prosperity, and good health.

Like many other flowers the clover was adopted by the Greeks and Romans to mark festive occasions—as garlands to grace the banquet halls and as "wine for merriment." English and American poets have expressed their appreciation in verse. Perhaps the most oft-quoted are Emily Dickinson's words:

> The pedigree of honey
> Does not concern the bee;
> A clover, any time, to him
> Is aristocracy.

41

Vermont chose a clover for its state flower, and gourmet cooks everywhere use it in the kitchen for its unique honeylike flavor. Perhaps a bee could best describe the taste of this flower. Those of you with vivid memories must remember strolling through the fields in the carefree days of childhood and sucking the nectar from the clover.

Always gather clover blossoms on a dry day. Thoroughly wash and dry them.

To prepare them for winter use place brown paper on a cookie sheet and spread the blossoms out on it. Set in a hot dry place out of the direct sunlight, or put them in your oven with the door open and the temperature set at the lowest heat possible. Check after 15 minutes to see if they crackle when pinched; if not, return to the oven. Keep a close watch so they don't become overdry and lose their color.

CLOVER TEA

Pour a pint of boiling water over a handful of clover blossoms (either fresh or dried) and allow to steep for 5 minutes. Strain and serve.

CLOVER OMELET

An excellent breakfast offering is an omelet with clover filling. Make your favorite recipe and just before folding over add 1 tablespoon clover petals and a teaspoon of honey per serving.

CLOVER BUTTER

A delightfully delicate spread for tea sandwiches.

  2 **tablespoons clover petals**
  ¼ **pound sweet butter**
  1 **tablespoon clover honey**

Pull the petals from the flower head, measure, and blend into the butter along with the honey. Refrigerate about an hour before serving.

CLOVER VINEGAR

Fill a pint jar with clover blossoms. Heat to the boiling point 1 3/4 cup vinegar and 3 tablespoons clover honey and pour into the jar containing the blossoms. Cover the jar and shake gently. Stand in a cupboard for 4-5 days. Strain.

IRISH "CLOVER BREAD"

This is a staple long remembered by visitors to Ireland. Dry the clover as discussed earlier in this chapter and when baking bread add about 1 tablespoon per loaf.

Dandelion

The dandelion originated in Ancient Greece, and is considered to be one of the bitter herbs of the Old Testament. Today dandelion still evokes bitterness in many gardeners, who find it almost impossible to rid their lawns and gardens of its so-called golden glory. Coming to America by way of Europe, the name dandelion is believed to be a corruption of the French *dent de lion*, or the Greek word *leontodon*—both meaning lion's tooth. The leaves of the plant certainly do bear resemblance to the jaws of the beast.

The botanical name for dandelion—*Taraxacum*—is a Greek word meaning "remedy for disorders." The American Indians called it "strong root" and utilized its strength medicinally. The Italians have always had a soft spot in their hearts for dandelion and often use it in a salad in place of chicory: the French still grow it commercially.

Some imaginative person once referred to dandelion as "the tramp with the golden head." Many of us remember the joys it provided in our carefree days of youth. The fluffy seed head carried a message of love, if you whispered the words before blowing off the fluff in the right direction of your beloved. If you worried about the weather you would watch to see if the down dropped off without wind—then rain was inevitable. And everyone's childhood memories must include picking dandelion bouquets for Mother.

There's a lot more to this ubiquitous weed than being a persistent nuisance. The Russians have been experimenting with its milky juice as a possible source for a rubber substitute. It has long been regarded as a tonic, and scientific experiment confirms the belief that it is beneficial to the health of the liver and kidneys. It is a good source of vitamins A, B, C, and E, and also contains calcium, potassium, magnesium, and iron.

The next time you yank up a handful keep in mind the homage due this golden tramp, carry it carefully to the kitchen, and enjoy its culinary uses. John Evelyn, a great diarist at the turn of the eighteenth century, wrote at length (in *Acetaria*) about the virtues of salads, and almost all his recipes included dandelions.

Dandelion greens and the flower buds may be cooked and served like spinach. Melted butter, salt and pepper to taste complete the dish, which makes a nice accompaniment for sausage.

Dandelion buds and leaves also make an excellent salad. Use a good French dressing, with a touch of garlic, salt, and pepper. Or add dandelion buds and young leaves to your favorite tossed salad.

The very young dandelion buds, fried in butter, taste similar to mushrooms. The leaves offer a pleasantly bitter taste.

Always select tender young dandelion buds and tender young leaves. They are often referred to as a spring tonic because the heat of summer toughens them and one must wait until the following spring unless your grocer carries cultivated dandelion.

Thoroughly wash the buds and leaves before using.

DANDELION SANDWICHES

Spread thinly sliced whole-wheat bread with butter. Place 4-5 very young tender leaves on the bread. Pull the dandelion petals from the stem and calyx of one or two partially opened flowers and sprinkle over leaves. Top with another slice of buttered bread.

DANDELION TEA

Pour 1 pint of boiling water over a handful of well-washed leaves and petals. Steep for 5 minutes. Strain. Many people find this soothing for an upset stomach.

DANDELION COFFEE

The roots of dandelion should be dug up in the fall and dried. Wash the roots thoroughly and spread out on a screen in a hot dry place for several days. These may be ground for making a coffee substitute.

DANDELION WINE

(An old Woodring recipe)
Gather the dandelion flowers on a dry sunny day. Use the petals only. Hold the flower by the stem and calyx and pull the petals from it. Drop the petals into a crock. Do not allow any part of the stem or "milk" to get into the container.

> 4 quarts boiling water
> 2 quarts flower petals

1 lemon
1 orange
1 cup raisins
1 small chunk ginger root (optional)
3 pounds sugar
1 ounce yeast on a slice of bread

Pour water over flower petals and let stand 4-5 days. Strain. Add the thinly sliced peel and the juice of a lemon and an orange, raisins, and ginger root and sugar. Boil 20 minutes. Return to the crock and let cool. Add the yeast on bread. Stand in a warm place for 3-4 days. Strain. Let stand 2-3 weeks. Decant and bottle.

Store 4-6 months before using. Tastes like a light sherry.

LUNCHEON DANDELION OMELET

2 servings

4 eggs
½ teaspoon water
2 tablespoons butter
4 tablespoons dandelion buds (sautéed)

Whip the eggs about 30 strokes with the water. Put butter into the omelet pan, and when it foams tilt pan so all sides of pan are coated. Quickly add eggs and stir in circular motion until the liquid sets. Just before folding over add dandelion buds, which have been sautéed in butter about 2-3 minutes. Crumbled bacon is a good garnish.

DANDELION SALAD GOURMET

4 servings

Garlic clove
  3-4 cups raw dandelion leaves
16-24 dandelion buds
    3 tablespoons salad oil
    1 tablespoon lemon juice
  1½ tablespoons vinegar
Salt and pepper
   ½ teaspoon chopped tarragon
   ½ teaspoon chopped chervil

Rub a salad bowl with a cut clove of garlic. Tear the dandelion leaves into bite-size pieces. Add the buds. In a separate bowl combine the oil, lemon juice, vinegar, salt, and pepper. Pour over the salad and add the tarragon and chervil. Toss gently. Sliced ripe olives may be added if desired.

WILTED DANDELION SALAD

4 servings

4-5 slices bacon
1 beaten egg
1 teaspoon dry mustard
2 tablespoons cornstarch
2 tablespoons sugar
4 tablespoons water
5 tablespoons vinegar
Salt and pepper to taste
4 tablespoons light cream
3-4 cups dandelion greens
2-3 dozen dandelion buds

Fry bacon until crisp; drain, reserving fat. In a double boiler over boiling water combine the egg, mustard, cornstarch, sugar, water, vinegar, salt, and pepper. Stir constantly until it thickens. Then add cream and 1 tablespoon bacon drippings. Blend, then add 2 strips of crumbled bacon. Pour over dandelion greens and buds and toss. Add remaining crumbled bacon.

Day Lily

The Chinese enjoyed the day lily long before the written word, and earliest records tell of the plant's use as food. An herbal from the T'ang Dynasty, about A.D. 650, informs us that "it quiets the five viscera [heart, lungs, kidneys, stomach, and liver], reduces worry and benefits the mind."

In China day lilies are a cultivated crop and do not grow hither and yon in back yards and along the highways and byways as they do here in America. They are not ordinary fare for the Chinese farmers, but are a cash crop and must be sold. New York City statistics show over 4,000 pounds of dried day lilies imported in a single year.

The next time you are in a Chinese grocery store ask for some "gum-jum" or "gum-tsoy," golden needles or dried day lilies. Soak the flowers in tepid water for 90 minutes, drain, and use the same as fresh blossoms.

Heavy smokers or others with an impaired sense of smell may find it hard to capture the delicate fragrance of day lilies. If you don't mind a little pollen on your nose from close whiffing you'll enjoy their sweet limelike aroma. If you break a flower off at its base you can suck the sweet nectar.

Day lilies are seldom attacked by disease or insects, and they have superior ability to withstand drought and compete with weeds. They multiply and bloom fervently without care or cultivation and are often regarded as wild plants. So prolific are their blooms that in spite of their name few people are aware that the glory of each blossom lasts but one brief day.

The sculptured elegance of day lilies endears them equally to flower fanciers who prefer the eighteenth-century Williamsburg style of mass arrangements and to proponents of the opposite in design—Japanese arranging. Why not take advantage of their abundance and use them as a centerpiece for your dinner table as well as in the stew or salad?

The flavor of day lilies is similar to that of chestnuts or beans—"with a touch of honey added." They contain vitamins and minerals and are high in protein.

Wash the blossoms thoroughly but gently, and drain. Remove the stamens and pistils.

Be careful not to overcook day lilies or they will become limp and exhausted.

We discovered that a day lily the day after its single burst of glory is at its peak of sweetness. Do not use the following day as it loses its texture and has an acrid taste.

Capture the delicate aroma and taste of day lilies by chopping the blossoms and adding to honey for two weeks. Strain the honey before using.

Chop the blossoms and add to scrambled eggs, omelets, or other egg dishes.

Place the buds in the juice of dill pickles and refrigerate overnight. Serve with cold corned beef, lamb, or tongue.

Sliced day-lily blossoms are a nice addition to a tossed salad.

DAY-LILY SOUP

6 servings

    5 cups chicken stock
    ½ cup minced chicken
       (or what may be garnered when making cooking stock)
1½-inch cube salt pork
    ¾ cup diced cooked potatoes
    2 tablespoons minced onion
    3 tablespoons minced celery
    ¼ teaspoon ginger
Salt and pepper to taste
    2 tablespoons flour
    2 tablespoons sherry
    3 tablespoons minced mushrooms (raw)
1½ cups chopped day lilies
    1 tablespoon parsley
    1 tablespoon soy sauce

Combine chicken stock, chicken, salt pork, potatoes, onion, celery, ginger, salt, and pepper, and cook 10-15 minutes.

Remove the salt pork; turn down the heat; add flour dissolved in sherry, mushrooms, day lilies, parsley, and soy sauce, and simmer 3-4 minutes.

DAY-LILY ASPARAGUS SALAD

4 servings

    1 dozen asparagus tips, about 4-inch lengths
    2 chopped day lilies
Chicory
    4 tablespoons salad oil
    1 tablespoon wine vinegar
    1 teaspoon lemon juice

1 tablespoon honey
Pinch of dry mustard
¼ teaspoon salt
Several grinds of fresh pepper
1 tablespoon capers

Cook the asparagus until barely tender (about 7 minutes) and cool it. Prepare the day lilies and cut into 3/4-inch lengths.

Place the chilled asparagus on a bed of chicory, sprinkle the day lilies over it and prepare a dressing with the following ingredients: salad oil, vinegar, lemon juice, honey, dry mustard, salt, and pepper. Shake well and pour the mixture over the salad. Sprinkle on the capers and serve.

DAY-LILY CHICKEN SALAD SPECIAL

4 servings

1½ cups diced cooked chicken
½ cup finely chopped celery
¼ cup chutney
1 tablespoon capers
1 tablespoon candied ginger
Salt and pepper

Combine the above ingredients with the following dressing:

¼ cup each lemon juice, mayonnaise, and honey
½ teaspoon tarragon
4 day lilies

On individual salad plates place some chicory. Spread open a day lily on each plate and top with chicken salad. (Prepare day lilies according to the directions at the beginning of this chapter.)

BUTTERED DAY LILIES

4 servings

8 day-lily blossoms
1 cup chicken broth
3 tablespoons butter
Salt and pepper to taste

Simmer the day lilies for 4-5 minutes in the chicken broth. Drain, add butter, salt and pepper to taste, and serve.

DAY-LILY TEMPURA

Makes approximately 2 1/2 cups

1 can beer (12 ounces)
1 cup all-purpose flour
Salt

Beat until frothy, then allow to sit for 3 hours.

Dust the prepared day-lily buds with flour, then dip into the batter and deep fry in oil (about 375°) until golden brown. Serve with the following avocado dunk:

2 avocados
¼ cup mayonnaise
1 garlic clove, mashed
2 tablespoons lemon juice
Dash of Tabasco

Peel and mash the avocados and combine with the remaining ingredients. A drop of green food coloring may be added for proper eye appeal. Chill at least one hour before serving.

Cut into 1 1/4-inch lengths. Fried day lilies make an interesting hors d'oeuvre.

DAY-LILIED DUCK

4-5 servings

- 1 duck, cut into serving pieces
- 4 tablespoons butter
- 2 tablespoons cornstarch
- 2 tablespoons soy sauce
- 3 tablespoons peanut butter
- ½ teaspoon nutmeg
- ½ teaspoon ginger
- 1 tablespoon grated orange rind
- Salt and pepper
- 1 cup sliced mushrooms
- 2 cups day lilies (whole or chopped)

Place duck in water to cover along with an onion studded with several cloves, a bay leaf, and salt. Simmer for 45 minutes. Drain and dry duck. Strain broth and reserve 2 1/2 cups. Sauté duck in butter until golden brown. Combine cornstarch and soy sauce and add to broth; stir over medium heat until smooth and thickened. Then add peanut butter, nutmeg, ginger, orange rind, and salt and pepper to taste. Continue stirring and when broth starts simmering add mushrooms and day lilies and cook for 3-4 minutes. Pour over duck on a heated serving platter.

DAY-LILY SAUSAGE TARTS

4 servings

    4 tart shells
    ½ pound sausage
    ½ pound mushrooms, sliced
    1 tablespoon minced onion
    1 cup day lilies, chopped
    ¼ cup and 1½ tablespoons butter
    1 tablespoon Madeira wine
    1 tablespoon chopped chives or parsley
    ½ tablespoon lemon juice
Salt and pepper
1½ tablespoons flour
    1 cup cream

Prepare and bake tart shells. Cook sausage. Place mushrooms, onion, and day lilies in skillet in which 1/4 cup butter has been melted. Sauté 2-3 minutes. Remove from heat, add drained sausage, wine, chives, lemon juice, salt, and pepper, and stir enough to blend well.

Prepare a roux of 1 1/2 tablespoons butter and the flour and slowly add cream, stirring until thickened. Add mixture from skillet, blend well and correct seasonings.

Fill pastry shells, sprinkle with chives. Place in oven for 5-10 minutes so they are hot for serving.

CHICKEN-DAY-LILY COMMOTION

4 servings

    4 tablespoons butter
    2 boned chicken breasts, thinly sliced, raw
    1 cup sliced mushrooms
  2-3 cups day lilies (1-inch pieces)
   ½ cup chopped onion
   ½ cup snow peas (1-inch lengths, diagonally cut)
  1½ tablespoons cornstarch
   ¼ cup chicken broth
    2 tablespoons soy sauce
   ½ teaspoon ginger
    2 tablespoons dry sherry
    1 tablespoon honey
Salt and pepper

In a large skillet melt butter, add sliced chicken, and cook 3-4 minutes, stirring to prevent sticking. Add mushrooms, day lilies, onion, snow peas, cornstarch dissolved in broth, soy sauce, ginger, sherry, honey, and salt and pepper to taste.

Keep up the "commotion" in the skillet for 3-4 minutes or until ingredients are fork tender, but not exhausted. Serve immediately. Good with rice.

PORK WITH DAY LILIES

4 servings

¾ cup onion rings
3 tablespoons butter
1 clove garlic, mashed
8 very thin slices of pork
1 tablespoon cornstarch
2 tablespoons soy sauce
¼ teaspoon powdered ginger
1 tablespoon Madeira wine
Salt and pepper to taste
1½ cups chopped day lilies

Sauté onions in butter until translucent. With a slotted spoon remove the onions and reserve. To the remaining butter add the garlic and pork slices; cook quickly on both sides. Remove the pork to a warm serving platter.

Stir the cornstarch into the soy sauce until smooth, then add to the pan juices along with ginger, wine, salt, and pepper. Stir until thickened and clear. Add the chopped day lilies and reserved onions and pan stir for two minutes over medium heat. Pour over pork and serve.

Elder

Some sources claim the wood of the elder tree was used for Christ's cross; others believe Judas hanged himself on an elder tree, and many superstitions have grown out of these stories.

The "spirit of elder" was prominent in European folklore and almost all gardens were planted with at least one elder in it to ward off evil. Since it was believed to be bad luck to uproot or cut them down, there are many very old trees around. In many Scandinavian countries people refuse to accept furniture or any objects made of elder wood.

In this country most of our elders are of a more bushlike formation. The American Indians had already discovered the virtues of elder when the white man arrived. Their whistles were whittled from the wood; they made use of it for medical reasons and enjoyed elder flowers as salad, as fried food, as seasoning, and in drinks.

The elder blooms abundantly in flat, massive bunches of white, honey-scented flowers. The taste is likened to sweet muscat grapes used in muscatel wine. After enjoying the many culinary possibilities you'll agree that at least one, or more, elder bush is needed in every garden—whether you believe in its efficacy against witches or not. You will have your own source of vitamins growing close by and soon your culinary enthusiasm for it may bind you to the believers who think it is bad luck to cut the elder down.

Elder flowers grow in clusters and the outer ones open first. Examine the clusters carefully and choose the ones with all flowers opened. Handle very carefully as they bruise easily. Very gently but thoroughly wash and drain them.

To dry for tea they should be spread out on a screen without touching each other. Place in a warm dry place for several days. Use the dried flowers sparingly as the drying process seems to intensify the flavor.

Place 2 teaspoons of dried blossoms in a teapot and add 1 pint boiling water. Allow to steep before serving.

ELDERBLOW WINE

As a child I was sure that elderblow wine must be the prettiest in the whole world, because of its lovely name. My grandmother's "Receipt Book" included this recipe.

- 6 **pounds sugar**
- 3 **gallons water**
- 1 **quart elder blossoms**
- 1 **Baker's yeast cake**
- 3 **pounds raisins**

Boil sugar and water until sugar is dissolved and pour over blossoms in a crock. Cool, then add yeast and raisins and let stand 9 days. Strain and return to the crock. Let stand in a cool dark place for 4-6 months. Strain and bottle.

ELDER-FLOWER VINEGAR

Elder flowers
White vinegar

Dry the elder flowers thoroughly. Then place in a jar. Heat the vinegar to the boiling point and pour to cover flowers. Put lid on the jar and let stand in the back of the cupboard about 10 days, shaking occasionally. Strain and bottle.

Very good with fruit salads (especially apple), or served in a cruet with pork roasts.

ELDER-FLOWER PANCAKES

Add elder-flower sections and a little grated lemon peel to your favorite pancake mix.

ELDER-FLOWER FRITTERS

Break flower head into small clusters, discarding stemmy parts. Pour a little brandy into a flat dish and allow clusters to stand in it at least 15 minutes.

Prepare a batter of the following:

1 can beer (12 ounces)
1 cup all-purpose flour
Salt to taste

Blend these ingredients well and let stand for 2 hours before using.

Heat oil to about 375°F. Dip blossoms into the batter and fry until golden brown.

Dust with powdered sugar and serve at once.

ELDER-FLOWER DUCK

6 servings

  1 duck
Salt and pepper to taste
½ cup currant jelly
¼ cup honey
  1 cup elder blossoms
¾ cup orange juice

Prepare the duck for roasting, rubbing inside and out with salt and pepper. Place in an open pan in a 325° oven.

In a saucepan, over medium heat, combine the other ingredients, stirring until well blended. Use this sauce to baste the duck about every 15 minutes. Roast about 25 minutes per pound, or until tender.

Place the duck on a serving platter, pour over it any remaining sauce, and garnish with a sprig of elder flowers.

Gardenia

The gardenia, a symbol of "secret untold love," was named for Dr. Alexander Garden, an eighteenth-century naturalist and physician.

> "My mind lets go a thousand things,
> Like dates of wars and deaths of kings"
> THOMAS BAILEY ALDRICH

—but the sweetness of a single gardenia can vividly recall high-school proms, soft spring nights and the first stirrings of romance. Why not recapture such poignant moments of the past by serving gardenias?

GARDENIA FRITTERS

4-5 servings

½ bottle beer (6 ounces)
½ cup flour
 1 teaspoon sugar
Pinch of salt
 1 cup gardenia petals
Powdered sugar

Combine the beer, flour, sugar, and salt and let stand for 3 hours or more.

Wash and dry the gardenia petals, dip in powdered sugar, then into the batter and cook in deep oil at 375°F. until golden.

To serve, sprinkle with powdered sugar, cinnamon sugar, or with Grand Marnier. Serve with coffee on a romantic night.

CANDIED GARDENIAS

See page 5.

Gladiolus

According to legend this regal flower had a tragic beginning. A wicked old man chopped down a sacred tree, killing the wood nymph who lived there; from her blood the gladiolus sprang forth.

"Gladiolus" is derived from the Latin word *gladius*, a short sword used by the Romans. Its name was inspired by its sword-like leaves. In Europe the flower is often referred to as "sword flower."

A fertile field for the hybridists, there are hundreds of species, offering every color and shade of the rainbow except a true blue.

The flower's flavor is similar to that of lettuce, and a red flower chopped up for a tossed salad satisfies the eye appeal when tomatoes are not at their best. Various shades add color to fruit salad also.

They make interesting containers for any mixture. A gladiolus flower may be filled with chicken, egg, or tuna salad. And don't overlook using these flowers to hold dips at cocktail parties. Handsomely arranged they make a dramatic centerpiece on the table.

Remember always to wash the flowers thoroughly but gently.

Hollyhock

The hollyhock is one of our oldest-known plants and has been a favorite for many centuries, especially in China, where hollyhocks originated. Like many plants of ancient origin they were discovered, lost, and reintroduced several times before becoming established. Thus they are sometimes said to have originated in Turkey, Syria, or Greece.

Althaea, hollyhock's generic name (from *althaia*, Greek), means to heal, and old herbals tell of their use in diuretics and cough remedies. When they reached England the leaves were used in a concoction for reducing the swelling in the hock (ankle) of a horse. They were believed to have come to England from the Holy Land, and thus holy-hocks and later hollyhocks became established.

No old-fashioned garden is complete without these tall, stately flowers nodding in the background, and many a grandmother is remembered for the delightful hollyhock dolls she created.

Hollyhock flowers, with the coarse, seedy center removed, make attractive containers. An artistic and unusual centerpiece for a cocktail party can be created with them. Cover a plate (I like an old-fashioned cake plate with a footed base) with crisp watercress. Arrange various-colored flowers on this, and fill each with a cocktail dip—such as caviar, liver pâté, blue cheese, etc.

Lavender

Here's your sweet lavender,
Sixteen sprigs a penny,
Which you'll find, my ladies,
Will smell as sweet as any.
OLD LONDON STREET CRY

Lavender is so strongly associated with London and sachet that many people forget it grows abundantly in America as well as in Spain, France, and other Mediterranean countries. Lavender's history goes back to Biblical days, when the Virgin Mary was said to include it among her favorite flowers. *The Greek Herbal of Dioscorides* (a first-century Greek physician) extolled lavender's medicinal virtues. The Romans cherished the flowers for festive occasions to enhance their food and to perfume the banquet halls.

Thriving on chalky soil, the lavender grown in England is considered more aromatic than species grown elsewhere, and the English have long recognized its epicurean qualities and planted it in their culinary gardens. Queen Elizabeth I was said never to be without conserve of lavender on her table. Many a soup, salad, or stew was enhanced with a touch of lavender, and the Queen is said to have consumed countless cups of lavender tea (possibly for faintness or headaches). The palace gardeners were under strict orders to have the flowers available at all times.

Gardeners claim lavender plants improve the soil, herbalists praise lavender's antiseptic and medicinal properties, and martini worshipers predict its fame among their dedicated.

To prepare lavender you should break off small sprigs of flowers about 3 or 4 inches long, and thoroughly but gently wash and dry them.

Lavender may be dried for winter use for making tea by hanging small bunches upside down in a warm dry closet.

Lavender has a captivating taste that eludes description.

The English have long had the habit of serving their fruit salads on a bed of lavender and lettuce.

LAVENDER TEA

Pour 1 pint boiling water over 3 tablespoons flowers and let steep for 3-4 minutes before serving. Use half the amount of flowers when using dried ones.

LAVENDER MARTINI

There are fashions in food just as there are fashions in clothes and home furnishings. After testing this out on many martini drinkers, here is my prediction for a new fashion in martinis:

Make your martini with your favorite proportions. Use a small sprig of lavender as the garnish. The oil of lavender is quickly but subtly released by the alcohol, furnishing a new appetizing taste.

LAVENDER FRUIT

4-6 servings

3-3½ cups fruit (oranges, grapes, cherries, pears, bananas, etc.), cut into bite-size pieces
8 or more sprigs lavender
4 tablespoons Grand Marnier
2 tablespoons kirsch
1 cup champagne

Combine the fruit, lavender, Grand Marnier, and kirsch in a bowl. Blend gently and chill for 2-3 hours, gently stirring once or twice.

Before serving pour a cup of champagne over the ingredients, and additional sprigs of lavender may be added in a decorative manner.

LAVENDER VINEGAR

Place several sprigs of lavender in your vinegar cruet and let stand for several weeks. This is an especially good dressing for fruit salads.

LAVENDER JELLY

About 5 medium glasses

2¼ cups bottled apple juice
1 cup lavender flowers
3½ cups sugar
½ bottle (4 ounces) liquid pectin

(continued)

Place apple juice and lavender in a saucepan and bring to a boil. Cover and remove from the heat. Let stand for 15 minutes and strain. Return 2 cups of this juice to the heat, add the sugar, and stirring constantly bring to a full boil. Stir in the liquid pectin and bring to a rolling boil for 1 minute, stirring constantly.

Remove from the heat, skim off the foam, and pour into jelly glasses with a sprig of lavender in the bottom of each glass.

LAVENDER APPLE CRISP

4-6 servings

4   tart apples (medium size) in ¼-inch slices
1   tablespoon lavender flowers (half the amount if petals are dried)
½   teaspoon ground cinnamon
1   tablespoon lemon juice
3   tablespoons butter
½   cup brown sugar
½   cup white sugar
1   cup flour
½   teaspoon baking powder
1   egg
Pinch of salt

Combine the apples, lavender, cinnamon, and lemon juice in a baking dish. Stir gently until the apple slices are coated evenly. Dot with butter. Mix the sugars, flour, and baking powder together and then add the egg and salt. Spread this mixture over the apple slices and bake at 350°F. for 40-45 minutes.

Lemon, Lime, and Orange Blossoms

Oranges were mentioned in early writings of China about 500 B.C. However, lemons and limes, native to Southeast Asia, are not found in records until the Crusades (twelfth century).

The cultivation of citrus fruits moved along with the march of civilization to every part of the world where the climate was favorable, and there are a bewildering number of varieties.

The blossoms are similar enough in appearance and flavor to be used interchangeably. We will use the term "blossoms" and you may use whichever is available to you.

Wash the blossoms thoroughly but gently.

Lemon, lime or orange blossoms enhance: half grapefruit, fruit ices, citrus soufflés, warm sauces, liqueurs, molded salads, marmalade, champagne.

Use fresh blossoms as a garnish for cold soups; they are also nice with hot onion soup. Tuck a sprig of flowers and leaves onto the plate alongside the soup bowl.

For boiled onions, make a cream sauce and add blossoms before serving.

VINEGAR

Fill a pint jar with lemon, lime, or orange blossoms and cover with vinegar. After 10 days taste. If not strongly enough flavored, strain and replace blossoms with fresh ones.

CITRUS COOLER

Makes 2 tall drinks

⅓ cup rum
½ cup dry vermouth
1 tablespoon lime juice
2 tablespoons orange juice
1 tablespoon lemon juice
2 tablespoons sugar
3 ice cubes
Blossoms for garnish

Combine all ingredients except blossoms in a blender for 30 seconds. Dip the edge of serving glasses into citrus juice and then into sugar. Add crushed ice and pour in the cooler. Garnish with blossoms.

CITRUS TEA

Use about 5-6 blossoms (fresh or dried) per cup.
Steep 5-6 minutes.

CANDIED BLOSSOMS

See page 5. Use on custards, rice pudding, whipped cream, icing, etc.

LIME-BLOSSOM PUNCH

36-40 punch cups

¾ cup lime juice
1 cup honey
1 bottle gin (4/5)
3 quarts ginger ale
24 or more blossoms

In a ring mold put about 1/2 cup of water and half the blossoms. Place in the freezer. When frozen add additional blossoms and fill the mold with ice water and return to the freezer until serving time.

In a large bowl combine the lime juice, honey, and gin. Add 8-12 ice cubes and place in the refrigerator to chill. Also chill the unopened bottles of ginger ale.

Add the ginger ale to the gin mixture, blend well; add the blossom mold (or flowers in individual ice cubes) and serve.

ICED LEMON SOUP

4-5 servings

2½ cups chicken stock
  1 tablespoon cornstarch
  1 cup light cream
  3 egg yolks
Juice of 4 lemons
Grated lemon peel
Salt and pepper to taste
Blossoms for garnish

To 1/2 cup of chicken stock add the cornstarch and stir until completely dissolved.

Place the remaining stock and cream in a saucepan over medium heat. Stirring constantly, add the dissolved cornstarch and simmer until slightly thickened.

In a separate bowl beat the egg yolks. Gradually add a small amount of the hot soup, then pour the egg mixture into the pan of hot soup, add the remaining ingredients and blend well. Heat, stirring constantly until bubbles appear, but do not boil.

Chill overnight. Garnish with very finely minced parsley and lemon blossoms.

CITRUS CRAB SALAD

Makes about 1 cup dressing

Combine sections of grapefruit and crabmeat, serve on a bed of lettuce with a few blossoms sprinkled over the top. Use the following dressing:

¾ cup mayonnaise
¼ cup lemon juice
2 tablespoons white wine
Salt and pepper to taste

LEMONED VEAL

4-6 servings

1½ pounds thinly sliced veal
¼ cup lemon juice
2 tablespoons flour
Salt and pepper to taste
2 tablespoons butter
1 teaspoon grated lemon peel
½ teaspoon tarragon
1 tablespoon minced parsley
½ cup chicken stock
1 dozen blossoms

Marinate veal slices in lemon juice for at least one hour,

turning occasionally. Drain well, reserving the juice; dust with flour, salt, and pepper. Sauté in butter until golden on both sides. Remove to hot serving platter.

To the pan juices add grated peel, tarragon, parsley, and chicken stock. Stirring with a fork, loosen all the drippings in the pan; add juice left from marinating. Taste and correct seasoning. Do not boil. Pour over veal on the serving platter and tuck in about a dozen blossoms.

HONEYED CITRUS CHICKEN

4 servings

1 frying chicken, cut into serving pieces
1 teaspoon grated lemon peel
1 teaspoon grated lime peel
1 teaspoon grated orange peel
½ cup orange juice
½ cup lemon and lime juice
¾ cup honey
1 teaspoon dry mustard
Salt and pepper to taste
Melted butter
Blossoms

Marinate the chicken for several hours in a sauce made of all the ingredients except butter and blossoms, turning occasionally.

Brush each piece with melted butter (reserving the remaining sauce) and bake at 350°F. for 30 minutes. Turn and bake another 20 minutes longer, or until well done.

Boil leftover marinade, pour over chicken, and place under broiler for 5 minutes.

Garnish with citrus blossoms.

CITRUS SOUFFLE

6 servings

1 envelope unflavored gelatin
½ cup cold water
1 teaspoon grated lemon rind
½ cup lemon juice
4 eggs, separated
1 cup sugar
1 cup heavy cream
Fresh or candied blossoms

Sprinkle gelatin on cold water to soften. Grate lemon rind and extract juice.

Combine egg yolks, lemon juice, and 1/2 cup of the sugar in the top part of a double boiler. Cook over boiling water, stirring constantly until slightly thick and custardy. Stir in the gelatin and lemon rind. Cool.

Beat the egg whites until they hold shape, then add the remaining 1/2 cup sugar and beat until mixture forms peaks.

Whip the cream until it holds shape, fold in the blossoms, and combine all the ingredients gently. Pour into a 1 1/2-quart soufflé dish with a collar (use a 4-by-28-inch strip of brown paper and fasten to dish). Chill 3-4 hours. Remove collar before serving and top with additional blossoms.

Lilac

April is the cruelest month, breeding
Lilacs out of the dead land, mixing
Memory and desire, stirring
Dull roots with spring rain.

T. S. ELIOT

China is considered the lilac's ancestral home, and like many other flowers it reached these shores via Europe. It has found a favorite home in New Hampshire, where it reigns as the state flower.

To locate lilac bushes, journey into the old sections of a town. Once planted, the lilac thrives without attention, and having reached a peak of popularity in Colonial days lilacs can often be found guarding the sites of abandoned houses.

In France the lilac is a commercial crop. Millions of the little flowerets are candied and exported yearly.

Always wash the fresh flowers thoroughly but gently.

CANDIED LILACS

Our recipe for candying or crystallizing flowers (see page 5) will preserve their prettiness for all-year use. Break each individual flower from the stem before proceeding. They are most effective when used to decorate cakes, puddings, and other desserts.

LILAC ICE MOLD

Pour water to the depth of 1/4-inch in a metal ring mold. Arrange the individual flowers in an upside-down manner so they will be effective when unmolded in a punch bowl. Allow to freeze, then add additional flowers and ice water and return to the freezer until ready to use.

Marigold

No one ever sent his true love a bouquet of marigolds! But the marigold has been greatly revered through the years for its culinary, cosmetic, and medicinal qualities.

The Greeks called them gold flowers, and the Romans, claiming they bloomed the first of every month, chose "calends" (the first day of the month); hence *calendula,* the botanical name for the herb species.

In medieval days when devils and demons were feared, people liked to associate flowers with the Virgin Mary. They believed by constant association with the flowers they could ward off evil. These particular golden flowers were called Mary's golden and became marigolds.

Marigolds are rooted in myth. One is the story of the four wood nymphs who fell in love with Apollo, the sun god. The nymphs became so jealous of one another they began neglecting their duties to Apollo's sister, the goddess Diana. She turned them into four dull-white marigolds, which distressed Apollo, but his only recourse was to send down his most brilliant rays to color them gold. Diana angrily decreed that yellow should forever after denote jealousy.

The exact date of the marigold's introduction to England is unknown, but references are made to it as early as the thirteenth century. Perhaps the eighteenth-century English put it to the best test—they used it as a love potion.

Marigolds decorated the robes of church statues in the Middle Ages, and since Shakespeare's time men have believed that "to look on marigolds will draw evil humors out of the head."

Early records indicate marigolds were brought to this country by the first settlers. Civil War works tell of marigolds "seasoned in lard" or marigold poultices being administered to soldiers' wounds. Joseph E. Meyer tells us in *The Herbalist* (first published in 1917 and now in its sixth printing) that marigolds contain vitamin C and phosphorous, good for teeth and bones. Indeed, Joseph Wood Krutch, in his *Herbal* declares "some of our most dramatic modern drugs, tranquilizers, antibiotics, etc., are derived from plants."

Poets through the centuries have sung of the golden beauty of the marigold. Gardeners love them for their easy growth and protectiveness for other plants. Their culinary virtues have long been honored by cooks. A medieval feast was described: "Marigolds seasoned the venison—roses graced the stew, and violets mingled with wild onion in the salad."

In the early days of this country dried marigold petals were sold in country stores, "out of a wooded barrel by ounce" just like other herbs.

Our great-great-grandmothers left us many recipes using marigolds in buns, rice, stews, cakes, broths, "drinkes," pickles, and "possets and pottage." Dutch chefs famous for their soups and stews acknowledge the marigold as their secret ingredient. Many wine and cordial recipes today use marigolds as the base.

You can save money by replacing the saffron on your herb shelf with dried marigold petals. Like saffron, which is used mainly for its yellow coloring, marigold petals impart the same golden hue and "pleasantly bitter taste."

To prepare marigolds: Pull entire petals from the stem, and

as you hold them firmly in your hand, with scissors cut off the white (or pale greenish) "heels," as this could give a bitter taste if not removed. Wash petals thoroughly but gently and drain well.

To dry marigold petals: Wash and dry the whole blossoms. Prepare by removing petals and cutting off the white heels. Spread the petals out thinly on brown paper on a cookie sheet and place in a barely warm oven. Too much heat will spoil their coloring. The petals may be dried outside by placing them on a screen located in warm air currents, but not in the direct sun.

Consider pulverizing some dried petals and placing them in a salt shaker for handy use.

All recipes use fresh marigold petals unless otherwise noted.

Eggs and marigolds make a very nice alliance. On a dull rainy day scrambled eggs seem to completely lack personality. So "put the sunshine into the frying pan." When the eggs are partially cooked add chopped fresh marigold petals. Use approximately 1 teaspoon chopped petals per egg. Remember to scramble eggs by slowly and gently lifting them from the bottom and sides so the liquid can flow to the bottom. Avoid constant stirring and remember that the heat in a skillet will continue cooking eggs after removed from the heat, so they should not be left standing in the pan.

Any cold green vegetable salad is enhanced both in flavor and appearance with a sprinkling of chopped fresh marigold petals.

MARIGOLD PARTY STICKS

4-5 servings

4 tablespoons butter
4½ tablespoons grated sharp cheese
1-1½ tablespoons pulverized dried marigold petals
¾ cup all-purpose flour

¼ teaspoon salt
Pepper to taste
 1 egg yolk
 2 tablespoons cold water

Blend the butter, cheese, marigold petals, flour, salt, and pepper. Combine egg yolk and water and stir into flour mixture. Refrigerate for several hours.

On a lightly floured board, roll out to 1/4-inch thickness; cut into strips 4 inches long by 1/2 inch wide. These can be twisted before being placed on an ungreased cookie sheet, or left straight. Bake at 400°F.—watching closely so they do not get too brown, which happens suddenly—for 10-12 minutes.

MARIGOLD CHEESE SOUP

6 servings

¼ cup butter
½ cup each minced celery and green peppers
¾ cup each minced onions and carrots
 4 tablespoons flour
 1 quart chicken stock
 3 cups grated Cheddar cheese
Salt and pepper
 3 tablespoons minced marigold petals
 1 cup milk
 1 cup cream
 2 tablespoons sherry
Chopped chives or parsley
Additional petals

Melt butter and sauté celery, green peppers, onions, and

carrots for 12 minutes. Add flour, constantly stirring, and slowly add stock, stirring constantly until slightly thickened.

Lower heat and slowly add cheese, stirring gently. Add salt, pepper, marigold petals, milk, cream, and sherry. Heat but do not boil.

Garnish with finely chopped chives or parsley and a single marigold petal. Pour into a tureen for serving and place watercress and marigold flowers around the tureen.

MARIGOLD CUCUMBERS

3-4 servings

Peel and thinly slice cucumber, sprinkle with 1/2 teaspoon salt, and refrigerate for about 1 hour.

Drain off the liquid that accumulates. Add:

> 1 **thinly sliced scallion, including green part**
> 1 **teaspoon chopped fresh marigold**
> **A liberal amount of freshly ground black pepper**
> ¼ **cup white vinegar**
> 3 **tablespoons each water and salad oil**
> **Dash of Tabasco (optional)**

Blend and refrigerate until serving time.

MARIGOLD FONDUE

4 servings

1 pound Swiss cheese, grated
2 tablespoons flour
2 tablespoons minced marigold petals
Salt and pepper to taste
Pinch of nutmeg
1 garlic clove
1 cup dry white wine
4 tablespoons kirsch

Place grated cheese, flour, marigold petals, salt, pepper, and nutmeg into a paper bag and shake well to combine. Rub the cooking pan with a cut clove of garlic, allowing it to remain in the pan. Add wine and bring to the boiling point. Remove the garlic clove. Slowly, while stirring constantly, add the cheese mixture. When it starts to boil remove from the heat, add the kirsch, and serve at once with cubed French bread for dunking.

MARIGOLD QUICHE

6 servings

½ pound bacon
1 nine-inch pastry shell
½ pound grated Swiss cheese
4 eggs
2 tablespoons flour
½ tablespoon salt
1½ tablespoons marigold petals
Pinch of nutmeg
Pinch of cayenne

(continued)

2 cups milk
2 tablespoons butter

Fry the bacon until crisp, and drain. Crumble and add to the pastry shell along with the grated cheese. Make a custard by whipping the eggs, flour, salt, marigold petals, nutmeg, cayenne, milk, and butter. Pour over the cheese and bacon and bake in a 375° oven for 40 minutes.

CONFETTI EGGS

3-4 servings

6 eggs
⅓ cup milk
2 tablespoons butter
Salt and pepper
2 tablespoons each finely chopped green pepper, marigold petals, onion, and tomatoes

Break the eggs into a mixing bowl. Add the milk and use a fork to blend thoroughly. Place the butter in a frying pan to melt. Tip the pan so the bottom and sides are well coated. To the eggs add salt and pepper, chopped green pepper, marigold petals, onion and tomatoes. Blend gently and pour into the frying pan and proceed in your normal way to scramble eggs.

We usually allow 1 1/2 eggs per person (with the extra half added if it comes out uneven) but you must decide in accordance with the size of the appetites you are feeding.

A pinch of crushed dried marigold petals is a treat sprinkled over fried or poached eggs.

Fresh or dried petals may be added to soufflés and omelets.

GOLDEN CRABMEAT

4 servings

½ cup chopped fresh marigold petals
2 cups crabmeat
¼ cup finely chopped celery
1 tablespoon finely chopped scallions or chives
1 tablespoon finely chopped parsley
1 teaspoon capers
½ cup sour cream
1 tablespoon lemon juice
1 tablespoon dry white wine
Dash Tabasco
Salt and pepper to taste

Combine marigold petals, crabmeat, celery, scallions, parsley, and capers.

In another bowl mix sour cream, lemon juice, wine, Tabasco, salt, and pepper.

Blend together the two mixtures. Correct seasonings and chill. Serve on crisp greens.

GOLDEN VENISON STEAK

4-5 servings

¼ pound butter
1½-2 pounds venison steak
½ cup flour
¾ cup red wine
1 cup tomato paste
1 cup chopped onion
½ cup chopped carrot

(continued)

½ cup chopped celery
2½ tablespoons Worcestershire sauce
Salt and pepper to taste
1 cup chopped marigold petals

Melt butter in skillet; brown meat and reserve. Stir flour into remaining butter until roux is formed. Stir in wine, tomato paste, onion, carrot, celery, Worcestershire, salt, and pepper. Blend well over heat and return venison to sauce. Cook in oven at 325°F. until fork tender (approximately 90 minutes).

Then stir in marigolds. Turn off oven and let stand in oven another 5 minutes before serving.

MARIGOLD RICE

4-5 servings

3 tablespoons butter
¼ cup minced onion
½ pound rice (a scant cup)
2-3 tablespoons minced marigold petals (1-2 tablespoons if crushed dried are used)
2 cups chicken stock
Salt and pepper to taste

Melt butter in a heavy pan; sauté onion until translucent, add rice and sauté until each grain is well coated. Sprinkle the marigold petals on the broth to soften and then add to the rice mixture along with salt and pepper. Cover and simmer about 20 minutes.

ZUCCHINI, MARIGOLD STYLE

4 servings

¼ cup butter
1 pound zucchini
1 scallion
½ teaspoon lemon juice
1 garlic clove
2 tablespoons soy sauce
1½ tablespoons chopped marigold petals
Salt and pepper

In a skillet melt the butter and add the zucchini, very thinly sliced, and finely chopped scallion. Stir so the butter coats both ingredients; add the lemon juice and garlic; cover and simmer 3-4 minutes. Blend in the soy sauce and marigold petals and return to the heat for another 5 minutes, or until the zucchini is softened but not exhausted. Remove the garlic clove and add salt and pepper to taste before serving.

MARIGOLD ONIONS

4 servings

Prepare and cook about 1 1/2 pounds small white onions until almost tender (approximately 20 minutes). Drain and place in a lightly buttered casserole.

Combine:

3 tablespoons butter
2 tablespoons soy sauce
2 tablespoons coarse bread crumbs
1½ tablespoon chopped fresh marigolds
1 teaspoon chopped fresh parsley

(continued)

Sprinkle over onions. Bake about 10 minutes in a slow oven so sauce flavorings can permeate.

MARIGOLD MACEDOINE

12-18 servings

1½ pounds yellow squash
18 small white onions
1 medium head cauliflower
1 pound green beans
2 green peppers, cut in 1-inch strips
1 cup chopped marigold petals

Make the following marinade:

1 quart chicken stock
1¼ cups dry white wine
¾ cup vegetable oil
½ cup lemon juice
2 garlic cloves, minced
1 dozen peppercorns
1 tablespoon salt
½ teaspoon marjoram
½ teaspoon thyme
1 tablespoon chopped fresh parsley
1 tablespoon chopped marigold petals

Simmer the marinade ingredients 45-60 minutes, strain, return to heat, and bring to a boil.

Peel, cube, and cook the squash in the marinade until tender—8-10 minutes. With a slotted spoon remove the squash and reserve in a dish on the side. Simmer the onions in the marinade until tender—about 10 minutes. Place in a dish on the side. Next cook the whole head of cauliflower in the marinade about 20 minutes. Reserve. Cook the green beans (ends removed) 10-12 minutes. Reserve. Finally cook the green peppers until tender— about 5-8 minutes. Reserve.

Remove marinade from heat, add 1 cup chopped marigold petals, stir about 2 minutes, and pour some over each vegetable. Cover the dishes tightly (with foil and lids) and let cool. Place in refrigerator overnight before serving.

Arrange vegetables attractively on a large platter (cauliflower in center) and spoon marinade over. Place a few lemon quarters (each studded with 3-4 cloves) on the platter and add a light sprinkling of additional petals on the cauliflower.

CELERY MARIGOLD

4-5 servings

- 3 cups celery, pieces sliced about 1½ inches long on the diagonal
- 1 cup chicken stock
- ¼ cup chopped onion
- 2 tablespoons chopped green pepper
- 2 tablespoons chopped marigold petals
- Salt and pepper to taste
- White cream sauce
- Additional chopped petals

Simmer celery in chicken stock for 12-15 minutes. Do not overcook. Drain and pour into buttered casserole. Add onion, green pepper, and marigold petals. Stir gently to blend well. Add salt and pepper to taste.

Make your favorite white cream sauce and pour over other ingredients. Place in oven (325°F.) for 15 minutes. Remove from oven and garnish with additional chopped petals before serving.

MARIGOLD MUFFINS

Makes 1 dozen

¾ **cup milk**
1½ **tablespoons crushed dried marigold petals**
2 **cups sifted flour**
1 **tablespoon baking powder**
½ **teaspoon salt**
3 **tablespoons vegetable oil**
4 **tablespoons honey**
1 **egg**

Heat milk to boiling point; add crushed marigold petals. Into a separate bowl sift the flour, baking powder, and salt. Add oil to milk mixture. Stir and let cool to room temperature, then add honey and egg and combine with dry ingredients.

Fill muffin cups two-thirds full; bake at 400°F. for 20 minutes.

PARTY SANDWICHES

Makes 18 bite-size pinwheels

Blend well a 5-ounce package of cream cheese (room temperature) with 1 1/2 tablespoons Madeira wine and 1/2 cup finely chopped marigold petals.

Spread on thinly sliced bread (crusts removed). Place chopped watercress lengthwise along one edge and roll up. Place in a dish with the open edge down and refrigerate for 1 hour before serving. These may be sliced as pinwheels at cocktail time.

CRABMEAT-MARIGOLD SANDWICHES

Makes 4 sandwiches

1½ cups cooked crabmeat
1½ tablespoons finely chopped green pepper
3½ tablespoons finely chopped marigold petals
 ½ cup finely chopped celery
 1 teaspoon lemon juice
Salt and pepper
Mayonnaise enough to bind (½ cup)

Combine all ingredients and use as a sandwich spread.

MARIGOLD CUSTARD

6 servings

 4 eggs
Pinch of salt
 ½ cup sugar
 3 cups scalded milk
 ¼ teaspoon vanilla
Marigold petals
Nutmeg

Combine eggs, salt, and sugar; beat until lemon colored; add milk very slowly, stirring constantly. Add vanilla.

Butter 6 custard cups or a one-quart mold. Place 2 fresh marigold petals in each custard cup—or a dozen petals in the quart mold if used—and pour in liquid. Sprinkle with nutmeg. Set cups or mold into a pan of hot water. Place in a 350°F. oven. Bake until firm, about 35 minutes.

Marigold petals may be added to bread pudding also. Mince petals and add to custard before pouring over bread cubes.

MARIGOLD MINCEMEAT PIE

6 servings

1½ cups mincemeat
 1 nine-inch pie shell
 ½ cup chopped fresh marigolds
 1 tablespoon orange-flower water
 1 tablespoon orange liqueur
 3 eggs
 ½ cup sugar
 1 teaspoon vanilla
Salt
1¾ cups scalded milk

Place the mincemeat in the pie shell, then the marigolds, and sprinkle with orange-flower water and liqueur.

Beat until fluffy the eggs, sugar, vanilla, and salt, and slowly add the scalded milk. Pour over ingredients in the shell and bake in a 325° oven about an hour or until the custard is set.

Nasturtium

Despite the confusion over its name, and the mystery surrounding its true origin, the nasturtium has continued to bloom bountifully, endearing itself to all gardeners.

Xenophon tells us that nasturtiums were eaten by the Persians about 400 B.C.—long before they became acquainted with bread. E. L. Sturtevant's *Notes on Edible Plants* refers to the spread of these flowers from their native Persia to the gardens of Syria, Greece, and Turkey. Many years later Alice B. Toklas (Gertrude Stein's companion) combined nasturtiums with chervil, oil, and lemon juice for a salad based on a recipe from a Turkish cookbook published in 1862.

Some sources credit these flowers to the American Indian; nasturtiums and sunflowers were found by the early settlers as their covered wagons rolled west through Indian territory. Nasturtiums were often referred to as Indian cress. Joseph Wood Krutch tells us that American nasturtiums were mentioned in a sixteenth-century Spaniard's book on "the joyous news out of the New Found World."

The Peruvian Indians lost many treasures to the Spanish and English during the desperate gold-seeking days of the sixteenth century. Peruvian legend tells of a native carrying a bag of gold down a mountainside; as he was attacked by some treasure seekers he begged the mountain gods to take back the gold.

In the struggle that ensued the nuggets spilled onto the earth and there sprang forth luminous gold flowers—nasturtiums. The believers in this Peruvian origin also claim the high air in the Andes Mountains was so soft, pure, and clean that the penetrating fragrance of the flowers made one's nostrils quiver— hence the name "nasturtium" (it means "nose twister" and is derived from the Latin *nasus*, nose, and *toquere*, to twist). If ever a flower deserved a more congenial name it is the nasturtium.

Other sources hold the Ancient Romans responsible for the misnomer. They had an unpleasant cress which "twisted the nose" and applied the name to all cresses.

By the mid-sixteenth century these golden flowers flourished throughout Europe. John Gerarde tells us that they graced the gardens of Louis XIV. They were much heralded by John Evelyn in his *Discourse on Sallets*, and today they are still considered a sophisticated salad ingredient in Europe.

Linnaeus in the eighteenth century decided the plant was not a cress and gave it its generic name *Tropaeolum*. He associated the shield-shaped leaves and helmet-shaped flowers with trophies of war.

Cress or not, the taste of the nasturtium is almost always described as similar to that of watercress—with a drop of honey added. Snap off a flower and taste it. It is hard to describe— sweet but mildly pungent. One can understand why its association with the watercress family has lingered.

Attractive and tasty, nasturtiums are also healthful and protective. Research has shown that they are high in vitamin C and contain an herbal type penicillin that helps ward off infection. The flower pods (seeds), leaves, and stems are all edible— everything but the root.

Nasturtiums do not dry well. If you want to have their peppery taste available in the winter months, know that you will have to sacrifice some of their coloring.

For best results egg and cheese dishes containing these flowers should be served immediately. If they are left standing too long, a bitter taste sometimes develops.

Ulcer patients can safely use the crumbled dried petals as a substitute for pepper.

The late President Dwight D. Eisenhower included them in his highly prized recipe for vegetable soup. There are hundreds of fine vegetable-soup recipes, and if you have found one that pleases your family stick with it. But why not try following the late President's suggestion and add some nasturtiums the next time you make it? You will be quickly converted. Add a handful of chopped blossoms and stems to the soup for the last 10 minutes of cooking.

Sprinkle "flecks of gold" on your soufflés and all egg dishes whether boiled, poached, fried, or scrambled. There is an affinity between nasturtiums and eggs, and they provide a new zip to breakfast.

Fill an omelet with:

3 chopped blossoms
½ teaspoon each of pimento, parsley, and butter
Salt and pepper to taste

Cauliflower, broccoli, Brussels sprouts and other vegetables take on new interest when chopped nasturtiums are added to melted butter and dribbled over to enhance both the taste and appearance.

Add chopped nasturtium petals when cooking beef stew and tuck several blossoms on the serving platter to give special eye appeal to an old staple. In the seventeenth century it was common for nasturtiums to grace meat stews.

Chopped petals added to a jar of pickles add color; and sprinkled over celery sticks, cucumber slices, or potato salad they enhance both appearance and taste.

NASTURTIUM ROLL-UPS

24 roll-ups

12 slices white bread
 1 stick butter, softened
¾ cup chopped nasturtium petals
 2 nasturtium leaves with stems, chopped
 1 tablespoon honey
 1 teaspoon lemon juice
Salt and pepper to taste

Remove the crusts from the bread slices and roll with a rolling pin.

To the softened butter add the nasturtiums, honey, lemon juice, salt, and pepper, and blend well. Spread about a tablespoon of this mixture on each slice of bread and roll up like a jelly roll. Fasten with toothpicks and chill about 30 minutes before serving.

To serve, remove the toothpicks, slice each roll in half and place on a serving plate, surrounding a nasturtium on one of its leaves.

NASTURTIUM NIBBLES

Makes 1 dozen appetizers

½ pound pork tenderloin
½ cup chicken stock
 2 tablespoons raisins
 2 tablespoons almonds
 1 soda cracker
 1 tablespoon minced onion
 1 tablespoon soy sauce
Mayonnaise to bind

Salt and pepper to taste
Nasturtium flowers

Cook the pork in chicken broth until well done. Drain. Put through a food grinder along with raisins and almonds. Lastly, put a soda cracker through the grinder so all bits of pork, almonds, and raisins are freed from the blades.

Blend well with onion and soy sauce and enough mayonnaise to bind (about 2 tablespoons). Add salt and pepper to taste.

Remove the "centers" of the nasturtiums and spoon in some of the mixture. Fold in each petal, making little packets. Additional soy sauce may be served as a dip.

CLEAR NASTURTIUM SOUP

4-6 servings

1 quart chicken stock
8 nasturtium flowers, chopped
8 nasturtium leaves, chopped
½ cup chopped celery
1½ tablespoons chopped onion
1 sprig parsley
Salt and pepper to taste
Additional nasturtium flowers and leaves

Combine all the ingredients except the last and bring to a boil, stirring constantly. Turn down the heat and let simmer for 6-8 minutes. Strain and serve immediately.

Garnish each serving with a pinch of finely chopped nasturtium leaf and a single blossom. Tuck a leaf and a fresh flower, or two, onto the soup plate at the side of the bowl before serving.

A nasturtium blossom on a dab of sour cream is perfect garnish on cold soups.

NASTURTIUM SAUCE

3 1/2 cups sauce

Especially nice with lamb, tongue, and veal.

- 3 **cups vinegar**
- ¼ **teaspoon salt**
- ½ **teaspoon horseradish**
- 1 **garlic clove**
- 6 **peppercorns**
- 3 **cloves**
- 1 **tablespoon olive oil**
- ⅓ **cup honey**
- 2 **cups coarsely chopped nasturtiums**

Combine all the ingredients and bring to a boil while stirring gently. Turn down the heat and simmer 5 minutes. Pour into a jar and store (covered) for 2 weeks. Strain and keep in a cruet, handy for use.

PICKLED NASTURTIUM PODS
(A substitute for capers)

- 2 **cups wine vinegar**
- 1 **tablespoon salt**
- 8 **peppercorns**
- 1 **clove garlic (optional)**

Combine ingredients listed above and drop nasturtium seeds (pods) into a wide-mouth jar with the preparation.

Since many gardens won't yield enough pods at one time you may add additional ones over a two-week period. Then remove the garlic clove and seal for 3 weeks before using.

Some people prefer to soak the seeds for 2-3 days in a salt brine before dropping into the vinegar mixture.

NASTURTIUM VINEGAR

3 cups

Loosely fill a quart jar with nasturtiums. Pour cider vinegar over to cover them, loosely cap, and stand on a shelf for 2-3 weeks. Strain and bottle for use on meats and salads. A garlic clove, peppercorns, or shallots may be added, if you prefer a highly seasoned vinegar.

NASTURTIUM SALAD DRESSING

1 1/2 cups

- 1 cup mayonnaise
- 2 tablespoons lemon juice
- 2 tablespoons honey
- 1 tablespoon salad oil
- ¼ teaspoon dry mustard
- 4 nasturtiums
- 2 nasturtium leaves
- Pinch of curry powder

Place all ingredients in a blender and blend for 45 seconds.

GOLD-TOUCHED CUCUMBERS

4-6 servings

2 cucumbers
1 teaspoon salt
3 tablespoons sugar
⅓ cup white-wine vinegar
2 tablespoons minced nasturtium flowers
1 tablespoon minced parsley
Salt and pepper to taste

Slice the cucumbers, unpeeled, into paper-thin slices. Sprinkle with 1 teaspoon salt and let stand 30 minutes. Press with a wooden spoon against the side of the bowl and pour off liquid.

Add the sugar and vinegar and blend well. Refrigerate for another 20 minutes. Then add the minced blossoms and parsley and salt and pepper to taste.

Serve well chilled.

TOSSED SALAD WITH NASTURTIUMS

4-6 servings

Add about 1/2 cup chopped nasturtium petals to about 3 cups salad greens (any combination—lettuce, watercress, endive, etc.) and toss with your favorite dressing.

FRUIT SALAD NASTURTIUMS EXOTICA

4 servings

⅓ cup finely chopped nasturtiums
¾ cup French dressing

2 tablespoons honey
1 tablespoon rum
2 bananas
2 oranges
1 apple
¾ cup fresh pineapple
½ cup seedless grapes
¼ cup sliced pitted ripe olives
1 tablespoon finely chopped candied ginger

Chop the nasturtiums, add to the French dressing along with the honey and rum, and let stand.

Prepare and combine the above fruits (or a selection of your own) in bite-size pieces. Add the olives and ginger. Pour on the dressing. Gently toss and arrange on lettuce on salad plates.

Garnish with additional nasturtiums which have been sprinkled with French dressing and paprika.

NASTURTIUM-MUSHROOM SALAD

(A favorite with men)

6-8 servings

2 cups sliced raw mushrooms
½ cup chopped nasturtium flowers
4 cups mixed greens (Boston lettuce, watercress, chicory, endive)
French dressing

Prepare mushrooms and nasturtiums. Line a salad bowl with crisp mixed greens, add the mushrooms and nasturtiums and a good French dressing (see page 5), and toss and serve.

POTATO SALAD A LA NASTURTIUMS

4-5 servings

> 3 cups sliced potatoes
> 3 tablespoons minced onion
> 2 tablespoons minced nasturtiums

Salt and pepper to taste
Pinch each of chopped parsley, chives, and tarragon

> 3 tablespoons dry white wine
> 3 tablespoons tarragon vinegar
> ¼ cup beef broth
> 3 tablespoons oil
> 2 tablespoons mayonnaise

Boil potatoes in their jackets. Peel and slice into a bowl and add the onion, nasturtiums, salt and pepper, parsley, chives, and tarragon. Combine the wine, vinegar, broth, oil, and mayonnaise and pour over the warm potatoes. Toss gently and chill.

Line a salad plate or bowl with nasturtium leaves before adding the potato salad, and garnish with one or more flowers.

CRAB SALAD A LA NASTURTIUMS

4-5 servings

> 2½ cups crabmeat
> ½ cup finely chopped nasturtium petals
> 1 nasturtium leaf, finely chopped
> 2 tablespoons minced onion
> 2 tablespoons minced celery
> 1 tablespoon minced parsley

Salt and pepper to taste

Combine the above ingredients in a bowl. Then add a dressing made by combining the following ingredients:

⅓ cup salad oil
 3 tablespoons wine vinegar
¼ teaspoon minced chervil
½ teaspoon Dijon mustard
Salt and pepper to taste

Blend well and refrigerate about an hour before serving.
Serve in a lettuce cup with a very thin slice of lemon.

POLKADOT SCRAMBLE

3-4 servings

2 tablespoons butter
2 tablespoons finely chopped onion
2 tablespoons finely chopped green pepper
2 tablespoons finely chopped pimento
¾ cup corn (cut fresh from cob, if possible)
6 eggs
½ cup chopped nasturtiums (flowers and leaves)
Salt and pepper to taste

Melt butter in a skillet, add onion, green pepper, pimento,
and corn, and sauté for 3 minutes.

Beat eggs about 30 strokes; to the vegetables add the eggs,
nasturtiums, salt, and pepper, and scramble until the eggs are
set, but not dry.

NASTURTIUM COTTAGE-CHEESE DELIGHT

6 servings

Lettuce
4 chopped nasturtium leaves
1 pound cottage cheese
10-12 nasturtium flowers

Cover a salad plate with lettuce. Sprinkle over coarsely chopped nasturtium leaves. Place cottage cheese in the center of the plate and surround with nasturtium flowers.

If desired, chopped petals and leaves may be blended into the cottage cheese. Do this at the last minute as this combination should not stand too long before serving.

ASPARAGUS WITH NASTURTIUM SAUCE

Makes 3/4 cup sauce

Cook asparagus stalks until tender but still crisp. Drain and wrap in a tea towel while you prepare this tasty nasturtium sauce.

Combine the following ingredients over heat, being careful not to let the butter brown:

6 tablespoons butter
1 tablespoon lemon juice
1 tablespoon white wine
2 tablespoons minced nasturtium flowers
1 tablespoon minced parsley
1 tablespoon capers
Salt and pepper to taste

Arrange the asparagus on a warm plate and spoon on the sauce. If you have fresh ginger root available grate a little over the finished dish before serving.

NASTURTIUM SANDWICHES

Makes 2 sandwiches

1 three-ounce package cream cheese (at room temperature)
2 chopped nasturtium flowers
1 chopped nasturtium leaf
1 tablespoon mayonnaise
Salt and pepper to taste

Cream together all the ingredients until light and fluffy. Spread generously on thinly sliced pumpernickel bread (with crusts removed).

This filling should be made immediately before serving as it becomes bitter if allowed to stand.

Pansy

At one time pansies had a very sweet fragrance, but today we enjoy them for their fanciful faces. Lacking sweetness, they have no distinctive taste. Very gently wash and dry the flowers and take advantage of their merriment.

Artistically positioned in lemon Jell-O, pansies make an eye-catching salad. A tall fanciful mold, released onto a bed of watercress on a footed cake stand, can provide an interesting centerpiece for your table.

Pansies may be candied and used to decorate a cake. If the flowers are large it is best to candy each petal separately and reassemble when placing on the cake. They should be used immediately as they do not store well.

Rose

Millions of words have already been written about the mystique of the rose—its loveliness, beauty, allure, and romance. The rose is symbolic of beauty, youth, fidelity, friendship, appreciation, congratulations, sympathy, and ah yes, *love*. It seems to express all emotions!

It is hard to be objective about the rose. It has intrigued poets, writers, and philosophers, who have tried to explain its glory—Homer, Sappho, Confucius, Shakespeare, Milton, Burns, Browning, Rossetti, and Gertrude Stein, who concluded it could only be defined in its own terms ("A rose is a rose is a rose"). For centuries the rose has held a prominent place in poetry, literature, art, tradition, horticulture, and cuisine. As a symbol it has led men in conquest, migration, colonization, war, and peace. Yet the origin of this mighty flower of inspiration is surrounded in mystery. There are conflicting descriptions of the rose, some crediting it with thirty, some sixty, and some 160 or more petals; the legends surrounding the rose are as numerous as its ascribed number of petals.

Awed by its beauty, the ancients created many myths in trying to explain the rose. Venus is pictured with roses as she emerges from the sea—in tribute to her beauty. Tales of Dionysus and Bacchus also relate to the rose. Perhaps wine made from the rose was the inspiration of their fabled nights of merriment.

Later, in the days of Christian history, the rose became the symbol of the Virgin Mary. People surrounded themselves with roses in hopes of warding off evil spirits and protecting themselves against harm. The likeness of a rose adorned church furnishings and garments, and the rose window became an early part of Gothic cathedral architecture. The rosary, a string of prayer beads, had its beginning with the rose also. Legend tells us that Saint Dominic for many years paid daily tribute to the Virgin Mary with an offering of roses. One day when evil was about to beset him a heavenly light surrounded and protected him; in this vision the Virgin Mary appeared and wove the flowers into a garland which she placed around his neck—the rosary. Early rosaries were made of rose beads (directions follow on page 133) and a very lovely custom was established whereby a bride would send her wedding bouquet to a convent to have the flowers made into a rosary.

The long-drawn-out wars between the House of York and the House of Lancaster in England were fought under the sign of the rose. One side chose a red rose and the other chose a white rose and the conflict came down through history as the Wars of the Roses.

The rose and the nightingale have long been linked together, and from France comes the legend that the rose is red from the blood of the nightingale, forming an eternal alliance of the beauty of song and flower. Scandinavians have believed that elves colored the rose and man benefits from its special protection; in Germany ill omens were once connected with roses and you got rid of evil spirits by burning the fallen petals.

It is generally accepted that the rose originated in Persia, although everywhere it went it was claimed as a part of that country's heritage. From Asia Minor through Greece, France, and Spain it finally reached our shores, when Spanish priests brought the plants to the missions of California. Life there was very purposeful so they were probably introduced for nutritive and medicinal purposes. Today four of our states regard the rose as their state flower.

The rose, in a multitude of colors, forms, and varieties, has served man well. Medicinally, Pliny in his *Historia Naturalis* (about A.D. 75) listed more than a dozen remedies using the rose. Rose water is available today in drugstores everywhere. The rose is very rich in vitamins and minerals and the fruits of the rose, rose hips, are one of the best natural sources of vitamin C. During World War II when ships could not take citrus fruits to England, rose hips were collected and made into syrup, jams, and soups to provide the much-needed vitamin C. Today we can purchase rose-hip tablets in drug and food stores.

The rose is one of the tastiest and most versatile flowers in the kitchen, and I have well over one hundred recipes in my collection. Selecting the "best" ones has been a difficult job. Once you have worked with these suggestions and are familiar with the fragrance, flavor, color, and texture, you will probably experiment by adding a touch of rose to some of your own favorite dishes.

The more fragrant roses offer the most flavor. Roses vary in flavor and the darker ones have a stronger taste than the lighter shades. The old-fashioned varieties are the best choice since some of our new hybrids have little—if any—fragrance or flavor, and the petals tend to be on the tough side, and those grown in the garden are more desirable than the greenhouse varieties.

Wash thoroughly but gently. As with other multipetaled flowers, grasp by the stem and with the other hand pull the petals (en masse) from the calyx. Then, with scissors cut off the white heels (point of attachment to the stem), as this part is often bitter.

Rose water and candied rose petals are available at fine gourmet stores everywhere.

ROSE WATER

Some of our finest rose water comes from France (also the Near East) and I usually buy mine, as the process for making it is rather bothersome. However, for the purists and the adventuresome, with time and patience, here is the process.

Pour 1 quart water into a 3-quart pan and add about 2 quarts well-washed rose petals; place the lid on it and seal with tape, allowing a length of tubing (about 2 1/2 feet) to extend out at one point, being sure it is not in the water. Place the pan over low heat. Put the other end of the tubing into a glass jar. The steam will carry the vapors into the tube and then into the jar. At one point the tubing must be chilled to condense the vapors; I usually place several ice cubes in a tea towel and wrap around the tubing about midway.

In the Mid East a rose-water bottle is kept on the table and used much as we do the ketchup bottle.

The delicate flavor of rose water varies, so when using it always use the minimal amount and taste before adding more. Rose water loses some of its flavor during actual cooking, so always add at the end of the cooking process.

ROSE SYRUP

Makes 3-3 1/2 cups

½ cup water
2 cups sugar
1 cup light corn syrup
3 tablespoons rose water
Red food coloring

Boil water, sugar, and corn syrup, stirring constantly until it spins a thread when dropped from a spoon. Remove from the heat and cool. Stir in rose water and a drop or two of red food coloring for the desired shade.

Use on fresh fruits, puddings, ice cream, cakes, rice pudding, custards, canned peaches, and other desserts. Use in making cookies, cakes, and cooling drinks, or add a few drops to whipping cream.

Rose syrup is especially good on pancakes and warm bread pudding.

Rose petals and buds may be dried to use for tea. Place them on a screen in a warm, dry place for several days; or place them on brown paper on a cookie sheet in the lowest possible oven for an hour or so. Pinch the petals occasionally to see if they are dried and crackle.

ROSE TEA

Place a handful of well-washed buds or petals in the teapot and pour in boiling water. Allow to steep before serving. Buds may be dried for winter use.

ROSE VINEGAR

  2 cups white vinegar
  ½ cup sugar
  1 quart rose petals

(continued)

Bring vinegar and sugar to a full boil, stirring constantly. Add rose petals, cover, and remove from the heat. Let stand overnight and strain and bottle. You may add red food coloring if desired. It is best to prepare this recipe in an enamel pan.

OR

¾ cup cider vinegar
2 tablespoons honey
1 teaspoon rose water

Blend well and if desired add a drop of red food coloring. Let stand an hour before using.

Rose vinegar is excellent on fruit salad, cold lamb, chicken salad, crabmeat, or lobster.

PICKLED ROSEBUDS

Rosebuds to fill a pint jar (baby rosebuds are best)
½ cup sugar
2 cups white vinegar

Place washed buds in the jar. Dissolve the sugar in the vinegar over heat and fill the jar to the top. Seal and store in the cupboard for about two weeks before using. Serve with crab, lobster, or chicken salad or sandwiches.

ROSE BUTTER

In a glass dish place a layer of rose petals (the most fragrant), then half of 1/4-pound stick sweet butter (sliced lengthwise), another layer of petals, the rest of the butter, and then cover with petals. Cover tightly and allow to stand at room temperature, unless it is extremely hot weather, for an hour. Refrigerate. The next day remove the petals and cream the butter before using.

OR

Cream together 1 stick butter and 1 teaspoon rose water.

Rose butter may be used for tea sandwiches or spread on bread with thinly sliced white chicken meat or crabmeat.

ROSE JELLY

5 medium jars

- 2 cups bottled apple juice
- 1 quart prepared rose petals
- 3½ cups sugar
- 1½ tablespoons lemon juice
- 2 tablespoons rose water
- A few drops red food coloring (optional)
- ½ bottle fruit pectin (Certo)

Simmer apple juice and rose petals for 5 minutes, cover, and let stand off the heat for 15 minutes. Strain, add the sugar, lemon juice, rose water, and a few drops of red food coloring to the liquid and bring to a full boil, stirring constantly; add 1/2 bottle fruit pectin and bring to a rolling boil for one full minute. Remove from the heat, skim off the foam, and pour into glasses.

ROSE-PETAL JAM (cooked)

6-7 medium jars

- ¾ cup water
- 1¾ pounds sugar
- 1 quart rose petals
- 1½ tablespoons lemon juice
- 1 tablespoon rose water
- A few drops red food coloring (if necessary for good color)

Pour water into a saucepan, then alternate layers of sugar and petals. Add lemon juice, stir gently and bring to a boil; lower the heat and simmer for 15 minutes, stirring occasionally. Add rose water and a drop or two of red food coloring for an appetizing color, and continue to cook until thick like a conserve. To test whether it is firm enough, drop some from a teaspoon onto a cold dish.

ROSE-PETAL JAM (uncooked)

6 medium glasses

Our grandmothers used to crush rose petals in a mortar for this one. Lucky us, now a blender makes the job easy.

- 1 cup water (or strawberry juice, if possible)
- 2 cups rose petals
- 3½ cups sugar
- 1 tablespoon lemon juice
- 2 tablespoons rose water
- 1 package fruit pectin (Sure-Jell)

Put 1/2 cup water (or strawberry juice) into the blender

with the rose petals and blend for 12 seconds; slowly add the sugar, blending for about 20 seconds more.

In a small saucepan combine the remaining water, the lemon juice, rose water, and fruit pectin; boil for one full minute and add to the blender. Blend about 20 seconds and pour into glasses.

This method retains the full bouquet of the roses and no vitamin content is lost.

The jam will keep 4-6 weeks in the refrigerator or several months if stored in your freezer.

Rose hips are the red-orange berries that develop after the petals have withered and dropped off. They are extremely high in Vitamin C.

To prepare: Choose only ripe, red, undamaged rose hips. Wash and dry them thoroughly and with scissors remove the tops and tails. Split open and remove the seeds.

ROSE-HIP JAM (uncooked)
Substitute rose hips for petals in the above recipe, but increase the initial blending time to 30 seconds and follow the same directions.

ROSE-HIP JAM (cooked)

6 medium glasses

- **1 quart rose hips**
- **3 cups water**
- **1 tablespoon lemon juice**
- **4 cups sugar**
- **½ bottle liquid pectin (Certo)**

Boil the hips with the water about 15 minutes and puree by forcing through a sieve. Measure 1 3/4 cups of puree and add the lemon juice and sugar.

Bring to a rolling boil, stirring constantly. Add 1/2 bottle liquid pectin, boil hard for 1 minute, remove from the heat, skim, and pour into glasses.

ROSE-HIP TEA

Prepare a handful of rose hips; slightly crush with the side of a cleaver and place in a teapot. Pour in a pint of water and steep for 7-8 minutes before serving.

WATERMELON COOLER

Makes 1 drink

1 cup watermelon (seeded and cut in small cubes)
2 tablespoons rose syrup
3 ounces Vodka

If possible have all ingredients well chilled. Combine with 3-4 crushed ice cubes in a blender for 20 seconds at medium speed. Top with a rosebud, rose petal, or candied flower. Serve in a tall glass with a straw.

THE ROSEHATTAN

We would like to pass on a unique way (inspired by Women's Lib) to add a touch of the feminine mystique to a popular cocktail, the Manhattan.

First, we get rid of the "man," then select a truly feminine first name, "Rose," and, by substituting Rose for man, we create a "liberated" cocktail.

1½ ounces whiskey
¼ ounce dry vermouth
¼ ounce sweet vermouth
3-4 drops rose water
A candied rose petal

Shake the liquid ingredients with crushed ice and strain. Drop a candied rose petal into the glass as a garnish.

FRUIT WITH THE TOUCH OF THE ROSE

4 servings

Combine about 3 cups of a combination of several or all of the following fruits:

seedless grapes	pears
cantaloupe	pineapple
honeydew	mangoes
peaches	watermelon

Allow fruit to marinate about 1 hour in the refrigerator in the following dressing:

¾ cup champagne
1 tablespoon rose vinegar
2 tablespoons rose syrup

Garnish with chopped rose petals and grated lime peel.

ROSE CHAMPAGNE MOLD

12 servings

2 envelopes unflavored gelatin
½ cup water
½ cup sugar
1 bottle of champagne (4/5 quart)
8 or more rosebuds
3 cups seedless white grapes
Mint leaves
Additional grapes for center

For easy unmolding, rinse a ring mold with cold water, shake out droplets, and refrigerate until ready to fill.

Sprinkle gelatin over 1/2 cup water in a saucepan to soften.

Place over heat and stir until dissolved. Add sugar and stir until dissolved. Remove from heat and combine with champagne; refrigerate until slightly thickened (like egg white).

Pour about 1/2 cup into the mold and arrange four rosebuds in inverted positions so they will be effective when unmolded. Chill until firm. Combine the grapes and remaining rosebuds with the gelatin mixture. Pour another 1/2 cup of the mixture into the mold, being careful not to disturb the roses. Let it set and then add the remainder.

This can be unmolded on mint leaves, or mint leaves can be placed around the outside. Fill the center with additional grapes.

LOBSTER SALAD A LA ROSES

3-4 servings

Perfect for a ladies' luncheon.

- 2 **cups cold cooked lobster**
- 6 **tablespoons salad oil**
- 3 **tablespoons vinegar**
- ½ **teaspoon rose water**
- ¼ **teaspoon minced fresh tarragon (optional)**
- **Salt and cayenne pepper to taste**
- **Pickled rosebuds (see page 114)**

Marinate the lobster chunks in the other ingredients for at least an hour in the refrigerator. Serve on lettuce with a few additional pickled rosebuds tucked in.

CHICKEN A LA ROSE

4 servings

    2 chicken breasts, split
Generous pinch each of ginger, salt, and pepper
    4 tablespoons butter plus 2 tablespoons
    ½ teaspoon lemon juice
    ⅓ cup honey
    1 tablespoon rose water
    2 tablespoons chopped rose petals

Remove skin, wash and dry chicken, then rub with ginger, salt, and pepper. Melt 4 tablespoons butter in a sauté pan and when it starts to foam add the chicken and brown on both sides. Then place chicken in a casserole.

To the juices in the sauté pan add 2 tablespoons butter, lemon juice, honey, and rose water. Blend well over heat. Pour over the chicken, cover casserole, and bake at 325°F. until fork tender (about 30-40 minutes). Baste occasionally.

Place chicken on a serving platter, sprinkle with rose petals and spoon remaining juices over all.

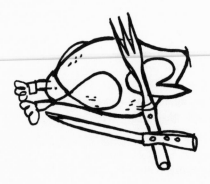

ROSE CHICKEN TARTS

6 tarts

Rich pastry
  1 can undiluted cream of chicken soup
  1 tablespoon minced onion
  1 tablespoon parsley
  1 tablespoon sherry
2½ cups diced cooked chicken
  1 tablespoon rose water
Salt and pepper to taste
Rose petals and 6 tiny roses

Line tart pans with a rich pastry. (I often use muffin tins.)
Allow enough dough to flute the edges. Bake. While the
shells are in the oven, in a pan on the stove combine the soup,
onion, parsley, sherry, chicken, rose water, salt, and pepper.
Stirring constantly, heat to boiling point. Cover and let stand
off the heat on the back of the stove.

Place rose petals in additional rose water to moisten. Remove baked shells, line with petals and fill with the hot mixture.
Dip whole roses in rose water and top each tart. If tiny roses
are not available substitute an additional petal on each tart.

EXOTIC LAMB CURRY

4 servings

1½ pounds lamb, cubed
  4 tablespoons flour
  4 tablespoons butter
  2 apples, peeled and chopped
  ¼ cup chopped celery

(continued)

2 tablespoons curry powder
3 thin slices lemon
2 tablespoons raisins
2 tablespoons brown sugar
1 cup each bouillon and water
¼ cup chopped walnuts
2 tablespoons chopped rose petals
4 tablespoons shredded coconut
½ cup sour cream
2 tablespoons rose water

Dredge lamb cubes in flour and sauté in butter about 10 minutes. Add apples, celery, and curry powder; blend well over heat. Add lemon, raisins, brown sugar, bouillon, and water. Blend well and cook over low heat about 45 minutes (covered).

Remove from heat, stir in nuts, rose petals, and coconut. Cover and allow flavors to blend for about an hour.

Add sour cream and rose water, heat thoroughly but do not boil, and serve with hot rice.

ROSE-GLAZED CARROTS

3-4 servings

2 cups sliced cooked carrots
2 tablespoons butter
2 tablespoons honey
1 tablespoon jelly (rose, currant, apple, or ginger)
1 teaspoon rose water
Salt and pepper to taste

Peel, slice, and cook carrots until tender. Drain. In a separate pan melt butter and add remaining ingredients. Simmer for

3 minutes and add carrots. Simmer 1 more minute. Let stand with a lid on the pan on the back of the stove off the heat until ready to serve.

ROSE-ACCENTED TEA SANDWICHES

24-32 tea sandwiches

- 16 slices bread (crusts removed)
- ¼ pound butter
- 4 tablespoons minced rose petals
- 1 tablespoon rose vinegar
- 1 tablespoon rose syrup (or honey)
- ½ cup minced chicken
- 2 tablespoons ground, toasted almonds

Salt and pepper to taste

Slice the bread very thin. Combine other ingredients for filling. Complete sandwiches, cut into quarters (or thirds) and top each tiny sandwich with a bit of minced parsley and additional minced rose petals.

MELON BALLS IN ROSE-RUM SAUCE

4 servings

With a melon scoop cut out small balls of cantaloupe, honeydew, and watermelon to equal about 3 cups. Chill. Combine the following ingredients for the sauce:

- ½ cup honey
- ⅓ cup rose syrup
- 4 tablespoons lime juice plus some grated rind
- ½ cup light rum

(continued)

Blend the ingredients well, pour over melon balls, stir gently, chill for at least an hour. During this time stir once or twice. May be served in a melon shell or in individual dishes. Garnish with chopped rose petals.

ROSY CUSTARD

4-5 servings

    2 cups milk, scalded
    ⅓ cup honey
    Pinch of salt
    3 eggs
    ½ teaspoon rose water

Heat the oven to 325°F.

Combine milk, honey, and salt. Beat eggs and blend in rose water. Add milk-and-honey combination. Pour into custard cups; place in a pan of hot water in the oven and bake for about 50 minutes.

Rose syrup (page 112) may be poured over the custard, or some finely chopped petals may be added before the dish goes into the oven.

BREAD PUDDING WITH A TOUCH OF THE ROSE

6-8 servings

    4 cups stale bread cubes
    3 cups milk, scalded
    6 eggs, separated
    1 teaspoon rose water
    ½ cup sugar
    ½ teaspoon nutmeg
    Pinch of salt

Set oven at 350°F.

Soak bread in milk. Meanwhile combine egg yolks, rose water, sugar, nutmeg, and salt. Blend well. Beat egg whites until peaks are formed. Gently fold egg whites into yolk mixture and pour over the soaked bread. With a fork stir lightly until well blended.

Place in a greased baking dish, set in a pan of water in the oven, and bake for about 45-50 minutes. Serve warm or chilled.

Rose syrup (page 112) is especially good on warm bread pudding, as the warmth seems to release the full essence of the rose.

ROSE OMELET (Dessert)

2 servings

    4 eggs
Salt
½ teaspoon rose water
    2 tablespoons chopped rose petals marinated in
    1 tablespoon each rose syrup (page 112) and Grand Marnier
Powdered sugar (for dusting)

Beat together the eggs with a pinch of salt; add rose water and beat again—about 30 strokes in all.

When butter in omelet pan foams, pour in the eggs. Keep tipping and rotating the pan to distribute the eggs evenly, and keep moving it so the eggs cook uniformly.

Use the petals in the syrup combination as filling and dust with powdered sugar.

ROSE SOUFFLE

8 servings

A cold, "easy to hold till the right time" type.

    6 **eggs, separated**
   ¾ **cup sugar**
  1½ **tablespoons unflavored gelatin**
    3 **teaspoons rose water**
    1 **tablespoon Grand Marnier**
   ½ **tablespoon grated orange rind**
    3 **tablespoons minced fresh rose petals**
    1 **cup heavy cream, stiffly whipped**
Candied rose petals to decorate

Beat egg yolks with sugar until thick and fluffy. Soften gelatin in rose water and Grand Marnier, dissolve over gentle heat, then stir into egg mixture. Place on ice and stir until it begins to set, add rind, rose petals and whipped cream; blend. Beat egg whites until stiff and fold in. Pour into a 1 1/2-quart soufflé dish which has been fitted with a collar so when collar is removed soufflé will rise about 2 inches above dish. Chill. Before serving remove collar and decorate with candied rose petals.

ROSE-PETAL FRITTERS

4-6 servings

½ cup beer (6 ounces)
½ cup flour
½ teaspoon salt
1¼ cups rose petals
Powdered sugar
Kirsch and/or rose water

Combine beer, flour, and salt and allow batter to stand for a couple of hours before using.

Wash and prepare rose petals. Be sure they are dry and dust with powdered sugar before dipping into batter.

Deep fry in oil at about 375°F. Drain on paper towels and sprinkle with rose water and/or kirsch and powdered sugar.

Serve warm at teatime or as a dessert.

ROSE FAMILY CREPES

1 dozen

Strawberries are of the rose family and the two flavors blend well.

Place in a blender:

3 eggs
1 cup milk
6 tablespoons flour
¼ teaspoon salt

Blend well, scrape down sides and blend again. Let stand 1 hour before using.

Heat crêpe pan; brush with butter. For a 7-8-inch pan, place about 3 tablespoons batter into the pan; keep tilting until pan is coated. Cook quickly over high heat, turning once to brown other side. Put aside on a clean dishtowel, folding it over between crêpes.

Combine:

½ cup rose-petal jam
½ cup strawberry jam (or fresh strawberries, sliced)
1 tablespoon rose water
1 tablespoon Grand Marnier

Spread some of this mixture on each crêpe. Dust finished crêpes with powdered sugar and ground toasted almonds mixed together.

ROSE TRIFLE

6 servings

Make this dessert in a glass dish so the mouth-watering combination of sponge cake, fruit, and custard can be seen.

1 sponge cake
3 tablespoons rose syrup
¼ cup Grand Marnier
½ cup rose-petal jam (see page 116)
1 cup sliced fresh strawberries
½ cup sliced peaches
2 cups vanilla custard
1 cup whipped cream
10-12 candied rose petals

Line the bottom of the dish with slices of sponge cake. Sprinkle with rose syrup and Grand Marnier. Spread with jam and then a layer of mixed fruits. Pour some custard over all. Repeat for two more layers. Then top with whipped cream and candied rose petals. Chill until serving time.

CANDIED ROSE PETALS OR FLOWERS

Prepare petals or tiny flowers and consult recipe on page 5.

ROSE-DROP COOKIES

3 1/2 dozen

2¼ cups sifted cake flour
¼ teaspoon salt
½ teaspoon baking soda
1½ teaspoons baking powder
½ cup shortening
1 egg, beaten
1 cup sour cream
½ cup brown sugar
4 teaspoons rose water
Light handful dried rose petals (optional)

Mix and sift first four ingredients; cut in shortening. Beat egg and add to sour cream and brown sugar; then combine with the flour mixture. Next add the rose water and if desired a handful of crushed dried rose petals to add a touch of color.

Drop by teaspoons onto a greased cookie sheet. Bake at 350°F. for about 15 minutes.

ROSE-ACCENTED CAKE

Substitute rose water (about 4 teaspoons) for part of the liquid in baking your favorite plain cake.

OR

Allow 2 or 3 tablespoons warmed rose syrup to seep into the top of the layers of cake (white or gold) before icing.

ROSE ICING

To frost a two-layer (8- or 9-inch) cake:

> ¾ cup rose syrup
> 3 tablespoons butter
> 1 pound powdered sugar (4 cups)

Blend together, then whip until light and fluffy. Add red food coloring (several drops) if you want a pink shade. Decorate with candied flowers, or tiny rosebuds and mint.

ROSE CREAMS

3 dozen

> 2 cups sugar
> ¼ cup light corn syrup
> ¼ cup milk
> ¼ teaspoon cream of tartar
> 1 tablespoon rose water
> Red food coloring

Combine sugar, syrup, milk, and cream of tartar. Place over low heat, stirring slowly, and bring to a boil. Place a lid on the pan for 2 minutes to allow the steam to dissolve any crystals which may have formed on the sides of the pan. Uncover and cook to the soft-ball stage (about 240° on a candy thermometer).

Allow to cool for 10 minutes, then add the rose water and a few drops of red food coloring. Beat until creamy. Drop from a teaspoon onto wax paper to cool.

These candies should be stored in an air-tight container.

ROSE BEADS

Old "stillroom books" listing the culinary and medicinal uses of the rose usually included directions for making potpourris and rose beads.

Pleasant fragrances are comforting—sometimes stirring childhood memories and sometimes stirring ideas of adventure and romance. Fragrance is such a part of the rose that I feel, as in the stillroom books, the directions should be included here.

Place 2 quarts of rose petals in a pan, barely cover with water, and simmer (do not boil) for 4-5 hours—until pulpy. Stir occasionally. Remove from the heat and let stand overnight. Sample a bit and see if it holds together. If it can't be shaped, add a little more water and simmer again. Some petals are tougher than others and take longer to soften.

When you can shape the pulp, roll it into little balls, pierce them with a thin toothpick, and string on wire to dry. It takes about a week, during which time move the beads about once each day so they don't stick to the wire.

If you would like black beads, simmer in an iron pot, preferably a rusty one.

The beads will shrink a little during the drying process.

ROSE POTPOURRI

- 1 quart dried rose petals
- 1 cup dried rosebuds
- 1 cup other dried flowers (choose a combination of violets, clove, carnations, borage, geranium, lavender)
- 1 ounce orris powder
- 1 teaspoon each cinnamon, nutmeg, cloves, mace, allspice
- 2 tablespoons dried orange or lemon peel
- 6-8 drops oil of roses

Combine the dried flowers and orris powder; stir gently with a wooden spoon. Combine the spices and tiny bits of dried peel, and blend all ingredients thoroughly.

Store in a sealed jar for 4-6 weeks to ripen.

Remember, the more fragrant the roses, the more fragrant your potpourri.

Rosemary

"There's rosemary, that's for remembrance;
pray you, love, remember."

SHAKESPEARE

The history of rosemary goes back hundreds of years. Legends tell us the flowers got their color when they were brushed by the blue robes of the Virgin Mary. I found record of their culinary use as early as 1594, when Sir Hugh Platt (*Delights for Ladies*) gave his "receipt" for candying rosemary flowers: ". . . take out your flowers with a skimmer, suffering the loose sirup to runne from them so long as it will . . . then boile all the sirup which remaineth and is not drunk up in the flowers."

According to the herbalists you should have rosemary in your garden for its protective powers and the raising of spirits. Rosemary will grow indoors if it is given a rich loamy soil and plenty of water and sunshine; restrict its size with constant use. Oh yes, a sprig carried to bed supposedly prevents nightmares.

The little pale blue flowers grow in clusters and give off a delicate spicy aroma. They have a pleasant resinous (piny) taste that can be termed sweet and savory. The freshness of rosemary goes nicely with poultry, lamb, and fish; it combines equally well with fruit salads, jellies, and biscuits. Keep in mind it is strongly flavored and should be used sparingly. Always wash the flowers gently but thoroughly before proceeding.

Prepare your favorite apple jelly and place a sprig of rosemary or a single flower in each glass.

Garnish serving platters of lamb, fish, etc. with the flowers.

ROSEMARY TEA

Place 2 tablespoons fresh flowers (only 1 tablespoon if dried) in a teapot, pour in 1 pint of boiling water and steep 3-5 minutes.

To dry the blossoms for tea, place the prepared flowers on a screen out of the direct sunlight, but in a hot dry spot, until they crackle when pinched.

ROSEMARY VINEGAR

Place a handful of flowers in a pint jar, fill with vinegar, shake, and let stand about 10 days. Strain. Pour this vinegar over additional fresh flowers if it is not flavorful enough and let stand another 10 days. Strain and use with game, fish, and fowl.

FRUIT SALAD "BY ROSEMARY"

Arrange your own choice of fruit on a bed of lettuce. Add rosemary vinegar to mayonnaise (or your choice of other dressing) by the taste method so you don't overpower other flavors. Tuck a few blossoms on the salad plate before serving.

CANDIED ROSEMARY FLOWERS

See page 5.

Squash Blossoms

The word squash comes from an Indian word meaning "eat raw" —*askutasquash*, an Indian name it deserves, as it was one of the common food crops when the white explorers first landed in this country. Archaeological research dates it back before the birth of Christ, seeds and rinds having been discovered in ancient ruins.

A prolific bloomer, a single squash vine produces dozens of blossoms. Consequently the Indians discovered they could enjoy the great delicacy of the flowers and still leave enough buds to mature and supply winter vegetables.

Squash blossoms resemble the vegetable in taste but the flavor is a little more delicate and perhaps sweeter. But you are dealing with a completely different texture.

The blossoms are best picked in the cool of the day. Wash them thoroughly but gently, and drain well before proceeding.

SQUASH-BLOSSOM SOUP

6-8 servings

- 3 **tablespoons butter**
- 3 **tablespoons flour**
- 2 **cups chicken stock**

(continued)

2 cups cooked and strained squash
1 cup chopped squash blossoms
½ cup chopped celery
¼ cup chopped onion
1 tablespoon chopped parsley
Pinch of rosemary
2 cups milk (or light cream)

Make a roux of the butter and flour; gradually add the chicken stock, stirring constantly to keep smooth. Add all the remaining ingredients except milk. Simmer 10 minutes, and add the milk (or cream), stirring constantly. Reheat, but do not boil.

SQUASH BLOSSOMS WITH SALAD

Toss your salad greens with chopped squash blossoms. All you need to add is a good French dressing. A few drops of honey may be added also.

SQUASH BLOSSOMS WITH EGGS

Add chopped squash blossoms when scrambling eggs. It adds a bit of sunshine to the breakfast plate. Depending on the size of the blossoms add 1 or 2 for each 4 eggs.

Prepare your favorite omelet and use blossoms sautéed in butter as the filling.

BUTTERED SQUASH BLOSSOMS

In a minimum amount of water gently simmer the blossoms about 1 minute or until fork tender and serve with salt and freshly ground pepper and butter. Allow 1 or 2 blossoms (depending on the size of the appetites you are feeding) per person.

BATTER-FRIED SQUASH BLOSSOMS

Makes 2 1/2 cups batter

Prepare our favorite batter for blossoms:

> 1 can beer (12 ounces)
> 1 cup all-purpose flour
> Salt

Beat until frothy, then allow to stand for 3 hours. Dip the blossoms into flour and then into the batter and deep fry in oil (about 375°F.) until golden brown.

To serve sprinkle with tomato sauce. Those with a sweet tooth may prefer a few drops of honey instead.

Leftover batter will keep 8-10 days in the refrigerator.

BLOSSOM-SMOTHERED DUCK

4 servings

> 1 duck, cut into serving pieces
> 1 bay leaf
> 1 small onion
> 2 tablespoons butter
> Salt and pepper

Simmer the duck in water to barely cover, along with the bay leaf and onion, for an hour or until tender. Drain the duck. Put butter in a skillet and brown the duck on both sides. Place in a casserole and salt and pepper the pieces.

(continued)

Make a sauce by combining the following:

2 tablespoons Grand Marnier
1 tablespoon soy sauce
½ cup orange juice
½ cup sliced mushrooms
Pan juices from browning duck
½ cup chicken stock
1 teaspoon grated orange peel

Simmer the sauce for 3 minutes; pour half over the duck. Return the other half to the stove and blend in:

1½ cups chopped squash blossoms

Stir while cooking until the petals are well coated, then pour over duck, place lid on casserole and place in a slow oven (about 300-325°F.) for 10 minutes. Remove lid, baste duck, and return to the oven for 10 more minutes.

Tulip

Historians generally agree that the tulip came from Persia. The accepted legend has it that a young man jumped from a cliff upon hearing a false report about the death of his beloved, and tulips sprang from the blood-stained earth.

The tulip early became a symbol of love and inspiration for poets and painters. In Iran today young men still express their love by giving tulips to their loved ones.

A Turk, shopping for perfume and rugs in Persia, is said to have dug up bulbs and taken them home to Constantinople. To the Turks the flower resembled a turban and the word in their tongue is "tulband," which in English becomes tulip.

Travelers from European lands were awed by the magnificence of these Turkish flowers and carried home the bulbs as presents. By the sixteenth century tulips bloomed in Europe, the bulbs selling for absurd prices. Occasionally someone mistook them for onions, only to learn later that he had consumed an extremely costly lunch.

During the tulip mania in Holland in the seventeenth century fortunes were lost as the bulbs became the objective of speculators and gamblers. People gave up their businesses, homes, lands, and belongings for unseen bulbs they hoped to sell to become rich. Archives record $2,000 being paid for a single bulb. Legislation was finally passed limiting their price.

As the supply of bulbs increased, the madness came to an end, but the Dutch saw the commercial value in raising tulips and Holland's magnificent tulip fields still supply the four corners of the world.

Tulips never reached a culinary high during the seventeenth century, when men were busy testing the edibility of flowers, because they were too rare and costly. But during World War II the Dutch reportedly warded off starvation by eating the flowers, bulbs, and stems of the graceful plant.

Tulips offer a combination of flavors, similar to peas and asparagus, and a variety of uses. Their size and shape make them wonderful containers for cocktail dips and salads. The chopped petals of tulips may be added to salad greens for a colorful touch. This is especially nice served in a brandy snifter at Easter, letting the colorfulness shine through. Do choose a combination of colors most pleasing or appetizing to the eye.

As containers for cocktail dips use tulips of different colors set on a bed of watercress.

I once served a spring luncheon using tulips filled with crabmeat. I chose a different color tulip for each guest. The table was so pretty and colorful that no centerpiece was needed.

To prepare the tulip: Cut early in the morning before the sun reaches the flower. Handle very gently, cupping it in your hand as you remove the pistils, etc. Still protecting its contour, wash thoroughly but gently. Lay it on its side to drain. Wrap a damp strip of paper toweling around the outside of it to help hold the shape and place on its side in the refrigerator until ready to use.

To stuff the flowers, hold the tulip in your hand and fill before placing on lettuce on a salad plate. The stickiness of the salad helps to hold the petals in position. Some tulips are unpredictable. Many a flower arranger has had his masterpiece threatened by a recalcitrant tulip and so we borrow his solution: "Drop some egg-white between the petals and let it set." This problem is the exception, but now you have the solution—just in case.

Texture is an important consideration here, so I suggest these fillings:

EGG SALAD

4 servings

      6 hard-cooked eggs
    ½ cup firmly chopped celery
      2 tablespoons minced green pepper
1½ tablespoons minced onion
      2 tablespoons chopped pickles
Salt and pepper to taste
    ½ cup mayonnaise
    ½ teaspoon chopped capers
Pinch of dry mustard
Pinch of curry powder

Chop the cooked eggs and add the other ingredients. Blend well and chill before stuffing tulips.

CHICKEN SALAD

6 servings

2 cups diced cooked chicken
½ cup crushed pineapple, drained
½ cup finely chopped almonds
½ cup white raisins
2 tablespoons lemon juice
.1 scant cup salad dressing
Salt and pepper to taste

Blend and chill the ingredients before filling tulips. (Finely chopped oranges and/or grapes may be substituted for some of the pineapple and raisins.)

Violet

Greek mythology tells us about the relationship of Zeus and the nymph Io. In order to hide her from his jealous wife, Hera, Zeus turned the lovely nymph into a white heifer. When Io's tears wetted the coarse grass upon which she was forced to feed, there sprang forth violets.

Another legend about violets has it that "Orpheus, being weary, stretched out upon a mossy bank to rest; and, from the spot where he laid down his lute sprang the first violets."

Throughout centuries the violet has been associated with modesty, innocence, and love. Its beauty appealed to Napoleon, and as his favorite flower it became a part of history as a political symbol. When he was banished to Elba, his last words were: "I will return with the violets in the spring." He returned in March (1815)—violet time—and his pathway was strewn with violets. Napoleon marked each anniversary of his marriage to Josephine by sending her violets, and when he died he was wearing a locket containing several faded violets from her grave. For many years the French Government banned any reproduction of the violet because it was a symbol of the Bonapartists.

Violets were among the first flowers to be cultivated for medicinal and food properties. Later they played a more aesthetic role. The story is recorded of a French gentleman who devoted thirty years of his life to growing violets. Each day he sent his mistress a fresh bunch; each night she plucked off the flowers and made a violet infusion, which she drank while toasting his devotion. Vitamins were unknown in those days and the dear lady never knew she was getting substantial daily doses of vitamin C. Her healthful glow most likely was attributed to love.

Violets are not just food for romantics and poets, but have been a favorite of gourmet cooks since the days of ancient Greece and Rome, when violet wine was drunk and the flowers used for syrups, salad, sweetmeats, and preserves.

In the eighteenth century French cuisine considered crystallized violets a *pièce d'occasion* and cultivation of violets for candying and use in perfume became big business. Gourmet food stores still stock candied violets from the shores of southern France.

The English have long regarded the violet as a cosmetic necessity for their fair ladies, both as a facial pack and steeped for tea. Queen Victoria commanded the royal gardener not to be without fresh violets for her tea, syrups, honey, jellies, etc.

Diamonds may be a girl's best friend but the gourmet cook chooses violets! Both the flowers and the leaves are edible, and they are high in iron and vitamins A and C. Their delicate flavor cannot be likened to anything else, but I know once you've tried them they'll soon become one of your favorites.

Always wash the flowers (or leaves) thoroughly, but gently, before using them.

Violets do not dry well, as they lose their texture. However, for tea I suggest you dry and store them—with a few leaves added. Spread the flowers and leaves on a screen and stand in a hot dry place until they are crunchy to touch.

Extremely effective visually and most simple to prepare are violets molded in lemon gelatin and served on violet leaves.

VIOLET WATER

Violets release their flavor and coloring very readily if placed in a glass jar or crock (do not use metal) and boiling water to cover them is added. Place a lid on the container and let stand overnight. (Use distilled water for best results.) Strain and use the liquid to color drinks, gelatin, icings, sauces, etc. If you prefer stronger flavor or coloring you may reheat the liquid and pour over a fresh batch of flowers.

VIOLET SYRUP

To each cup of violet water add 2 cups sugar and 3 tablespoons white corn syrup. Boil until it forms strings or drops as it falls from your stirring spoon (about 240°F. on a candy thermometer). It can be stored in a jar at room temperature. Violet syrup is excellent with ice cream, desserts, and lemonade.

VIOLET TEA

Use a handful of fresh or dried violets (and crushed leaves, if desired) for each cup. Pour boiling water over them and let steep for 4-5 minutes. Strain and serve.

This tea is high in vitamin C and will serve as an excellent pickup when you are tired.

CANDIED VIOLETS

See page 5.

VIOLET VINEGAR

Fill a jar firmly with violets and pour in heated white vinegar to cover. Put a lid on the jar and shake gently. Allow to stand 2-3 days until the vinegar has absorbed the flavor and color. Strain and keep on the kitchen shelf to mix into mayonnaise for fruit salads, crabmeat, etc. It imparts a very delicate flavor and coloring.

VIOLET JELLY

5 medium jars

  1½ **cups violet water** (p. 147)
   1 **tablespoon lemon juice**
  3½ **cups sugar**
   ½ **bottle fruit pectin (Certo)**

Combine the violet water, lemon juice, and sugar in a large pan. (You may make double violet water to use in making jelly. Pour your first batch of violet water over fresh blossoms and repeat the process.) Place over high heat and bring to a boil, stirring constantly. Stir in the fruit pectin and boil hard for one full minute, stirring constantly.

Remove from the heat and if you prefer a deeper coloring for eye appeal, add one or two drops of both red and blue food coloring.

Skim off the foam with a metal spoon and pour into glasses.

To some glasses add a rose-geranium leaf for additional taste and eye appeal.

VIOLET JAM

Makes 6 medium jars

1½ cups violet flowers
1½ cups water
3 tablespoons lemon juice
3 cups sugar
1 package fruit pectin (Sure Jell)

Put the violets, 3/4 cup of the water, and the lemon juice into your blender and blend at high speed for 1 minute. Add the sugar and blend another 60 seconds.

Stir the pectin into the remaining water and boil for a full two minutes, stirring constantly. Pour this hot mixture into the blender and blend another 2 minutes. Pour into jars and seal. Store in your freezer.

No vitamins are lost in this process and you retain the fresh flavor of the violets.

VIOLET MUSHROOM CAPS

2 dozen

Sauté 24 medium-sized mushroom caps in butter and drain on paper toweling.

Mix:

¾ cup sour cream
1 teaspoon lemon juice
1 teaspoon cognac (optional)
2 teaspoons chopped chives
2 teaspoons chopped violets

(*continued*)

Fill mushroom caps with above mixture and garnish each with a violet. You can also combine 1 teaspoon each cognac and lemon juice and dip in a violet to use as a garnish on each stuffed mushroom cap. Serve chilled.

CUCUMBER COOLS

20-25 canapé

Slice a peeled cucumber into 1/4-inch slices and marinate at least 1 hour in the following mixture:

¼ cup mayonnaise
1 teaspoon lemon juice or white vinegar
Pinch of garlic salt
½ tablespoon minced onion
Salt and pepper to taste

Drain. Pat dry one side of each slice and place (dry side down) on bread rounds and place a violet on top of each cucumber slice.

VIOLET CANAPES

Approximately 24 canapé

1 five-ounce jar pineapple-cheese spread
1 two-and-a-half-ounce can deviled ham
1 tablespoon Madeira wine
Pinch of curry powder
Pinch of garlic salt
2 tablespoons chopped violets

Mix the above, form into bite-size balls, and roll in minced parsley. Top each one with a violet.

SALMON PARTY BALL

Will serve a dozen or more guests

1-pound can (2 cups) salmon
1 eight-ounce package cream cheese, softened
1 tablespoon lemon juice
2 teaspoons grated onion
1 teaspoon horseradish
¼ teaspoon salt
¼ teaspoon liquid smoke (optional)
3 tablespoons snipped parsley
¾ cup chopped violets

Drain and flake the salmon. Combine the above ingredients and blend well. Adjust seasoning to taste. Chill at least 3-4 hours. Immediately before serving roll ball in additional violets to completely cover and stand on watercress, preferably on a compote dish.

EGG DELIGHTS

12-15 canapés

4 hard-boiled eggs (forced through a sieve)
1-2 drops Tabasco
Pinch of curry powder
Mayonnaise to moisten
Chopped violets

Spread on bread rounds or sliced celery root and top each with a fresh violet.

VIOLETS IN SOUP

Violets provide a striking garnish and combine nicely with almost all cold soups. They can be alternately spooned into soup dishes with jellied madrilène or consommé. Put a dab of sour cream in the center and top with a fresh violet.

Cold fruit soups are still considered unusual in America. However, once you indulge in these delicious and refreshing soups you will probably become a real devotee. You can copy the Scandinavians and serve cold fruit soups at either end of a meal, simply by altering the garnish.

Before a meal soup should be garnished with sour cream topped off with fresh violets. For dessert use whipped cream and top with either candied violets or fresh ones dipped in orange liqueur or lemon juice.

Many Europeans serve fruit soup hot if the weather so dictates.

JELLIED VIOLET CITRUS SOUP

4 servings

2 tablespoons unflavored gelatin
½ cup orange juice
2½ cups grapefruit juice
2 tablespoons sugar
½ cup lime juice
2 tablespoons orange cordial
½ teaspoon grated lemon peel
½ cup violets

Soak gelatin in orange juice for 3 minutes. Heat 1 cup of grapefruit juice and add gelatin mixture and stir until dissolved. Add sugar and stir until dissolved. Then add remaining ingredients except violets and chill. When the mixture is about the consistency of egg white beat with a wire whisk. Repeat several times during the chilling process.

Fold in violets before serving and garnish with whipped or sour cream and additional violets.

VIOLET PINEAPPLE SOUP

6 servings

4 cups pineapple juice
3 tablespoons quick-cooking tapioca
3 tablespoons sugar
½ teaspoon grated lemon peel
2 cups sliced strawberries or red raspberries
1 cup diced orange sections, or drained canned mandarin
   sections
2 tablespoons orange liqueur
½ cup fresh violets

Combine pineapple juice and tapioca and bring to a boil. Remove from heat and add sugar and lemon peel. Blend and cool to room temperature. Add fruit, orange liqueur, and violets. Chill. Before serving top each bowl with sour cream and a fresh violet.

POACHED SALMON AND VIOLETS

3 servings per pound of salmon

A poached whole salmon decorated with violets, cucumber slices, and minced parsley is a beautiful dish and an epicurean delight, which a novice can make with confidence, although it does take time and patience.

Simmer 15 minutes in a roasting pan (if you don't own a fish poacher) the following ingredients:

1½ cups clam juice
1 cup water
1 cup dry white wine
1 thinly sliced onion
1 bay leaf and a generous pinch each of thyme and parsley

Wrap whole salmon in cheesecloth and lower into the stock (court bouillon). If it does not cover the fish add enough water to barely cover it. Simmer about 4 1/2 minutes per pound.

Remove and cool well. Fish must be placed in the refrigerator for 2–3 hours before skin can be easily removed. The salmon now is ready to serve, but for a real gourmet touch I suggest that you glaze it before adding the garnish.

Make one pint of unflavored gelatin according to the directions on the envelope, using half court bouillon and half white wine for the liquid required. Allow to thicken slightly and pour over the fish and let set until firm. Cut off excess gelatin at the edges and garnish with very thin slices of cucumber topped with violets and finely minced dill or parsley.

VIOLET CHICKEN CURRY

4 servings

- 4 tablespoons butter
- 3 tablespoons finely chopped onion
- 1 tablespoon curry powder
- 1 tablespoon flour
- 2 cups chicken broth
- 1 apple, cored and chopped
- 2 tablespoons honey
- Pinch of ginger
- 1 tablespoon lemon juice
- 3 tablespoons shredded coconut
- 2 cups diced chicken
- Salt and pepper
- ¼ cup candied violets

In a saucepan melt the butter and sauté the onion until transparent. Stir the curry powder and flour into 1/4 cup of the broth until smooth, and add to the onion. Sauté 1 minute, stirring constantly. Blend in the remaining chicken broth slowly. Add the apple, honey, ginger, lemon juice, coconut, chicken, and salt and pepper, and let simmer for 10-15 minutes. Stir in candied violets when ready to serve.

A nice accompaniment is half an avocado filled with fresh pineapple, sprinkled with a tablespoon of violet water and topped with a fresh (or candied) violet.

VIOLETS WALDORF

8 servings

> 3 cups diced apples
> 1¼ cups diced celery
> ¾ cup slivered almonds
> Sugar to taste
> ¾ cup violets
>> 1 cup salad dressing (preferably half mayonnaise and half whipped cream)

Combine the above ingredients and serve on lettuce. Sprinkle additional violets over each serving, or make your own favorite Waldorf-salad recipe and add violets.

VIOLET VEGETABLE SALAD

10-12 servings

> 2 envelopes unflavored gelatin
> 3½ cups water
> 3 tablespoons honey
> 2 tablespoons lemon juice
> 1 tablespoon vinegar
> Salt and pepper to taste
> 1 cup violets
> 1 cup diced cucumber
> ¾ cup chopped celery
> ¾ cup chopped scallions (include part of the green tops)
> ½ cup sliced radishes

Soften gelatin in 1/2 cup of the cold water. Add 3 cups boiling water and the honey and stir until dissolved. Add lemon juice, vinegar, salt and pepper to taste. Refrigerate.

Prepare violets and raw vegetables and combine with gelatin when it begins to thicken. Pour into mold and chill until firm. Unmold on greens (preferably watercress) and garnish by sprinkling with additional violets. Serve with a good French dressing.

Cooked asparagus or green beans are a good addition, if proportions of other vegetables are reduced. Do not reduce amount of violets.

SALMON SALAD

1/2 cup dressing

Arrange salmon chunks on watercress. Surround with thinly sliced cucumbers. Sprinkle with lemon juice, salt, and pepper. Scatter violets and chopped chives over them and serve with this dressing:

6 tablespoons salad oil
2 tablespoons lemon juice
Salt and pepper to taste
1 tablespoon capers
Pinch of tarragon

A very simple but elegant salad:

On lettuce place avocado slices and sprinkle with lemon juice. Top with sour cream and fresh violets dipped in lemon juice.

VIOLET MUSHROOM SALAD

6-8 servings

 1 garlic clove
 2 cups raw sliced mushrooms
 2 heads Bibb lettuce
 ¾ cup violets
 1 tablespoon chopped chives
 ½ tablespoon minced parsley
Salt and pepper

Cut garlic and generously rub a bowl with it. Discard garlic; thinly slice the mushrooms into the bowl and refrigerate 30 minutes, gently stirring the mushrooms several times.

Place lettuce in a serving bowl. Gently combine violets and mushrooms and place on lettuce. Sprinkle with chives and parsley. Add salt and pepper to taste. Make an oil and vinegar salad dressing at the table according to your preference. Toss at the table.

This is a favorite salad with men.

VIOLET ORANGE SALAD

4 servings

Salad greens
 1 red Italian onion
 2 seedless oranges
 ¾ cup violets
 3 tablespoons good French dressing
Salt and pepper

Place crisp salad greens in a salad bowl. Slice thinly the onion and oranges. Arrange them alternately in a circle on the greens and place the violets in the center, with a few sprinkled about. Pour the dressing on just before carrying to the table and toss before serving.

OMELETS WITH OOMPH

The difference between an omelet which is plain fare and that which is a culinary triumph is the filling. Of course, the tender loving care with which it is made pays off too. A properly garnished omelet served with a flourish is a quick way to establish a cook's reputation. Flowers are the perfect enhancement.

I include here my way for the cook who is just adding the omelet technique to his repertoire. If you have developed your own successful method, use it; there are numerous methods and recipes.

Use 2 eggs per serving. For best results don't cook more than 4 eggs at a time.

To become an expert reserve a pan for omelets only. An omelet cannot be made in a sticky pan—the eggs must be able to slide around. A 7-inch or 8-inch skillet is a good size.

Place a dab of butter in pan to melt. Meanwhile, put eggs in bowl and beat with a fork about 30 strokes. They will be stringy but don't overbeat. Season with salt and pepper.

Tilt the pan so bottom and sides are coated with butter. As soon as foam has subsided quickly pour in eggs. Stir with a fork in circular motion and shift pan to and fro—just until all free liquid begins to set. Shake the pan so omelet stays free.

Place filling on omelet and, holding pan at a 45-degree angle over heat, with your fork quickly help fold omelet over and serve immediately. If allowed to stand it will toughen.

OMELET OOMPHS

Try these various fillings:

Fresh violets and grated lemon peel.

Diced crabmeat, chives, and violets, blended together with a few drops of sherry.

Red caviar, chopped walnuts, violets, and cognac.

Sour cream, violets, and grated lemon peel.

Chopped asparagus and violets.

Grape jelly and violets.

Whipped cream, violets (fresh or candied), and candied ginger.

Sliced strawberries and violets blended with orange liqueur.

(For dessert omelets I usually add 1/2 teaspoon sugar to the eggs and then sprinkle the finished product with powdered sugar and/or candied violets.)

THE SPECTACULAR COLD SOUFFLE—A LA VIOLETS

The cold soufflé, or mousse, as your grandmother used to call it, is rapidly gaining favor because it can remain in the refrigerator indefinitely without worry of collapse. It makes a very showy dessert.

Use a 1 1/2-quart soufflé dish (straight-sided) and make a collar by cutting a 4-inch strip of brown paper long enough to go around the dish. Fasten outside edge securely, allowing it to extend 2 inches above the top of the serving dish. When ready to serve, remove paper.

COFFEE-VIOLET SOUFFLE

6 servings

    1 envelope unflavored gelatin
¾ cup cold water
    2 teaspoons instant coffee
    4 eggs, separated
    1 cup sugar
Salt to taste
    1 teaspoon vanilla
    2 tablespoons coffee liqueur
    1 cup heavy cream
½ cup candied violets

Sprinkle gelatin on 1/4 cup of the cold water to soften. Dissolve instant coffee in remaining 1/2 cup water. Place egg yolks, coffee, 1/2 cup of the sugar, and salt in top of double boiler. Cook over boiling water, stirring constantly, until slightly thick and custardy. Remove from heat, stir in gelatin and vanilla and cool.

Beat egg whites until they hold a soft shape. Add remaining 1/2 cup sugar gradually and continue beating until mixture forms a peak. Beat heavy cream until it holds a shape and fold in 1/2 cup candied violets.

Gently combine all mixtures and pour into soufflé dish (with collar). Chill 2 or 3 hours. Decorate top with additional violets.

LEMON-VIOLET SOUFFLE

6 servings

   1 envelope unflavored gelatin
  ½ cup cold water
   4 eggs, separated
   1 cup sugar
Pinch of salt
  ½ cup lemon juice
   1 teaspoon grated lemon rind
   1 cup heavy cream
Fresh or candied violets

Sprinkle gelatin on cold water to soften.

Combine egg yolks, 1/2 cup of the sugar, salt, lemon juice and rind in the top of a double boiler. Cook over boiling water, stirring constantly until slightly thick and custardy. Stir in the gelatin. Cool.

Beat the egg whites until they hold shape, then add the remaining 1/2 cup sugar and beat until mixture forms peaks. Whip the cream until it holds shape and fold in the violets.

Gently combine all the ingredients. Pour into a soufflé dish (with a collar) and chill 2-3 hours.

Remove collar before serving and top with additional violets.

VIOLET-STUDDED SNOWBALLS

Allow 2 per person

Vanilla ice cream
Lemon sherbet
Orange liqueur
Candied violets

Before preparing this very simple but impressive dessert, decide exactly the number of servings you wish to make and very carefully choose the proper container to enhance the overall picture. A brandy snifter is especially nice, if you have one the right size.

Working quickly, place alternate scoops of lemon sherbet and vanilla ice cream in the glass container. Sprinkle orange liqueur onto each ball as you build the mound and stud with candied violets. Place in the freezer until serving time.

The vanilla ice cream balls may be rolled in coconut. If your ice cream is on the soft side, place on a cookie sheet in the freezer to harden before combining with lemon ice, etc.

Tangerine ice is a nice addition, or substitute for the lemon ice.

VIOLET-PISTACHIO PARFAIT

6 servings

½ cup water
1 cup sugar
Pinch of salt
2 egg whites, beaten stiff
1 teaspoon almond extract
Green food coloring
2 cups heavy cream
½ cup candied violets
½ cup chopped pistachio nuts

(continued)

Boil water, sugar, and salt until it forms a soft ball when tested in cold water. Beat egg whites to form stiff peaks, combine gradually, and continue to beat until about room temperature. Add almond extract and a couple of drops of green food coloring.

Whip the cream until stiff and fold in the candied violets and pistachio nuts. Combine with egg-white mixture. Pour into parfait glasses and freeze until firm. Top with additional whipped cream and candied violets and a fresh or candied mint leaf.

VIOLET-PINEAPPLE PARFAIT

6 servings

1 cup crushed pineapple (fresh preferably)
½ cup green crème de menthe
Vanilla ice cream
Candied violets

Combine drained crushed pineapple and crème de menthe. Alternate layers of ice cream and sauce with 2 or 3 candied violets until parfait glasses are filled. Freeze.

Top each with whipped cream and a candied violet and mint leaf.

VIOLET-LIME BOMBE
    Vanilla ice cream
    Candied violets
    Chocolate liqueur
    Lime ice

Line the sides of a bombe mold with vanilla ice cream. Stud generously with candied violets and sprinkle liberally with a chocolate liqueur. Then fill the center of the mold with lime ice. Place in the freezer.

To unmold, wrap the mold in a hot damp cloth for a few seconds. Turn onto a platter. Decorate with whipped cream and additional candied violets.

To serve cut in wedges. A tablespoon of Chéri-Suisse or crème de cacao sprinkled over each serving is a nice addition.

Woodruff

The principal use of woodruff is in the making of May wine. The best May wine comes from Germany, where woodruff grows along the banks of the Rhine in the Black Forest. Woodruff grows wild in many wooded sections of this country, and given a shady spot in your garden it will flourish in sandy soil with little attention. A pot of woodruff growing on the windowsill will fill your kitchen with the sweet smell of freshly mown hay.

The fragrance and flavor of the flowers are very closely allied; and the taste of woodruff is similar to lemons and vanilla blended together. Make this pretty white star-shaped flower a part of your culinary habits.

Gently but thoroughly wash the flowers before using.

WOODRUFF TEA

Allow 1 teaspoon woodruff to steep in a pint of boiling water for a long time—about 20 minutes.

WOODRUFF IN DRINKS

A flowering sprig is a nice garnish for a glass of wine, apple juice, or orange juice.

MAI BOWLE
(Waldmeister Bowl)

25-30 punch cups

- 1 **handful woodruff blossoms and leaves**
- 1 **cup super-fine granulated sugar**
- 2 **quarts Moselle or Rhine wine**
- 6 **ounces brandy**
- 1 **whole orange, quartered**
- 1 **bottle champagne (4/5 quart)**
- 1 **ice ring with woodruff flowers**

Place the woodruff blossoms and leaves in a large bowl, add the Moselle or Rhine wine, brandy, and orange, and refrigerate for 5-6 hours or more. Chill the champagne. Make an ice ring in a ring mold with some blossoms and a few leaves placed in the water.

To serve, put all ingredients including the champagne and ice mold into the punch bowl.

CANDIED WOODRUFF FLOWERS
See page 5.

Use sprigs of woodruff to dress up fruit salad and place a flower in the bottom of some jars of apple jelly for a different flavor and a floral accent.

Yarrow

Nicholas Culpeper, famous seventeenth-century astrologer-physician, claimed many virtues for this common plant which is regarded in many areas as a weed. In some European countries it is used in the making of beer. Yarrow has a spicy scent and is claimed to be beneficial to the digestive system; and it contains minerals and vitamins.

Very young tender yarrow flowers may be added to salads.

Yarrow tea made by pouring a pint of water over a small handful of blossoms is another delight.

Yucca

Yucca . . . desert candle . . . Spanish bayonet . . . moon candle . . . Adam's needle . . . or whatever you call it—a delightful culinary experience!

The American Indians were using yucca before the white man reached these shores. Fibers, or threads, were pulled from the edges of the leaves for use in sewing, and the beautiful blooms were used as food.

Yucca is similar to peas or asparagus in taste but the flowers offer a different texture from those vegetables.

To prepare yucca flowers: pinch off each individual flower and remove the hard center since it is not a good texture and sometimes is rather bitter. Wash the blossoms thoroughly but gently, and drain.

For salad marinate yucca flowers in a good French dressing. Chopped yucca petals go nicely in any tossed salad.

YUCCA SOUP

4-5 servings

   3 **cups soup stock**
   2 **cups chopped tomatoes**
   1 **small onion, chopped**
   2 **tablespoons green pepper, chopped**
   1 **clove garlic, minced**
Salt and pepper to taste
   2 **cups yucca flowers**
   1 **tablespoon sugar**
 ½ **cup peas**

Combine the soup stock, tomatoes, onion, green pepper, garlic, salt, and pepper. Simmer 30 minutes. Add yucca, sugar, and peas, and simmer another 10 minutes.

YUCCA TEMPURA

6-8 servings

   ½ **can beer (6 ounces)**
   ½ **cup flour**
   ½ **teaspoon salt**
1-1¼ **cups yucca flowers**
   ¼ **cup soy sauce**

Prepare batter of beer, flour, and salt and let stand for 2 hours or more. Place prepared blossoms in soy sauce to marinate. Shake off excess sauce before dipping into batter. Heat oil to 375°F. and deep fry yucca.

Serve with additional soy sauce for dipping.

They make nice appetizers.

CREAMED YUCCA

4-5 servings

2 tablespoons butter
2 tablespoons flour
1 cup milk
1 beaten egg yolk
1 teaspoon minced onion
Pinch nutmeg
Pinch thyme
Salt and pepper to taste
2½ cups prepared flowers

Make a roux of the butter and flour over low heat. Heat the milk and gradually add to the roux, stirring constantly to keep smooth. Remove from the heat and briskly stir in the egg yolk, minced onion, nutmeg, thyme, salt and pepper, and pour over blossoms in a serving dish.

The blossoms may be parboiled for 3-5 minutes, or you may serve the sauce on the raw flowers. I prefer the crispness of them raw.

Further Note to the Reader

FLOWERS IN WINE MAKING

The use of flowers in making wines has been greatly appreciated since the days of the Roman Empire. There are excellent books on wine making available today and I suggest that you consult one of them for the best procedures.

During my research I noted recommendations for use of the following flowers:

carnation	marigold (cordial)
chrysanthemum	orange blossom
clover	rose
dandelion	rosemary
elderblow	woodruff
lavender	

Childhood memories, and noting the well-thumbed pages on which dandelion and elderblow were written in old family "receipt books," prompted me to share these with you—in their respective chapters.

EDIBLE FLOWERS

The flowers used in this book have been carefully selected and checked.

It should be pointed out, however, that not all flowers are edible. Before you experiment with others by all means consult your local botanical garden, your county agricultural agent or public health official, or the national clearing house for poison control centers.

A few of the common garden flowers particularly to be *avoided* are:

azalea	rhododendron
crocus	jack-in-the-pulpit
daffodil	lily of the valley
foxglove	poinsettia
oleander	wisteria

SUPPLIERS

Rose water and orange-blossom water are available at gourmet food stores. Rose water is also available from your druggist.

Candied roses, rose petals, violets, lilacs, mimosa, and mint leaves are sold in gourmet food stores.

If these products are not available in your area, they may be ordered from

Le Bouquet
Box 11322
Fort Lauderdale, Florida 33306

Index

73 74 75 76 77 10 9 8 7 6 5 4 3 2 1